avocaderia

avocaderia

AVOCADO RECIPES FOR A
HEALTHIER, HAPPIER LIFE

alessandro biggi • francesco brachetti
alberto gramigni

Photography by Henry Hargreaves

HOUGHTON MIFFLIN HARCOURT

Boston   New York   2018

For information about permission to reproduce selections from this book, write
to trade.permissions@hmhco.com or to Permissions, Houghton Mifflin Harcourt
Publishing Company, 3 Park Avenue, 19th Floor, New York, New York 10016.

hmhco.com

Library of Congress Cataloging-in-Publication Data

Names: Biggi, Alessandro, author. | Brachetti, Francesco, author. |
Gramigni,Alberto, author. | Hargreaves, Henry, author.
Title: Avocaderia : avocado recipes for a healthier, happier life /
Alessandro Biggi, Francesco Brachetti, and Alberto Gramigni ; photographyby
Henry Hargreaves.
Description: Boston : Houghton Mifflin Harcourt, 2018. | Includes
bibliographical references and index.
Identifiers: LCCN 2018017533 (print) | LCCN 2018019119 (ebook) |
ISBN9781328499134 (ebook) | ISBN 9781328497932 (paper over board)
Subjects: LCSH: Cooking (Avocado) | Health. | LCGFT: Cookbooks.
Classification: LCC TX813.A9 (ebook) | LCC TX813.A9 B54 2018 (print) | DDC
641.6/4653—dc23
LC record available at https://lccn.loc.gov/2018017533

Cover illustration by Anna Resmini
Book design by Allison Chi
Food styling by Caitlin Levin

Printed in China

TOP 10 9 8 7 6 5 4 3 2 1

Dedicated to avo lovers
around the world

contents

ALESSANDRO

ALBERTO

FRANCESCO

introduction

——

NAME: Alessandro Biggi

TITLE: CEO

HOMETOWN: Modena, Italy

FAVORITE MENU ITEMS: Mediterranean Toast (page 49);
El Salmon (page 46) with egg; Avo-Mango Smoothie
(page 169)

NAME: Francesco Brachetti

TITLE: CEO/Director of Operations

HOMETOWN: Prato, Italy

FAVORITE MENU ITEMS: Quinoa & Friends (page 67); Avo-
Mango Smoothie (page 169); Greek Island Salad (page 68)

NAME: Alberto Gramigni

TITLE: Chef

HOMETOWN: Prato, Italy

FAVORITE MENU ITEM: Green Peas, Mint & Burrata Toast
(page 58); Guac Tots (page 130); Ginger-Mint Lemonade
(page 168)

ON AVOCADERIA'S OPENING DAY, we ran out of avocados after just ninety minutes—and things haven't slowed down since. Avocados stole our *corazón*—our heart—and as it turns out, we weren't the only ones. We now run through an average of two thousand avocados a week.

Back in 2016, we dreamed of opening the world's first avocado bar, a place where people could get healthy, avo-based meals—think smoothies, toasts, salads, bowls, and desserts—and we knew it had to be in New York. We walked around for a month looking for the right spot, and just before heading to the airport to catch a flight back to Italy, suitcases in hand, we walked into Brooklyn's Industry City. We were mesmerized by the energy of the space, a collection of enormous industrial warehouses that spanned an entire city block, including a food hall with communal dining. We knew this was exactly where we wanted to open our first Avocaderia outpost. Needless to say, we nearly missed our flight. Oops.

How did three native Italians end up serving food made with Mexican avocados in Brooklyn? That's easy. It started with . . . what else? An avocado toast. It was 2010 at New York City's Cafe Gitane, a retro café famous for its see-and-be-seen hipster vibe and Moroccan-influenced food. That's where Alessandro had his first avocado toast, an experience that would save him from endless nights of unhealthy takeout food.

Six years later, Alessandro was living in Seattle, where he was working long hours. He didn't know how to cook, but he liked to prepare simple things, so he started making himself avocado toast with a little lime and salt—and loved it. It made him feel healthy, and then the idea of opening a business based on fast-casual healthy food hit him. He wanted to serve food that not only looked good, but made people feel great. The first person he shared his idea with was Francesco. Not only was Francesco his best friend, he was also living in Mexico at the time. What better place to learn about avocados? So we threw around the idea of opening up an avo-centric spot together, and our enthusiasm only grew the more we talked about it. We knew if we opened this place, it would be so much more than just an eatery: It could have the power to change people's eating habits and—not to be drama queens, but—their lives, too. We'd show them that a healthy lifestyle is the best way to live.

We first met in 2006 in Milan, where we were studying finance at the prestigious Bocconi University. Alessandro spotted a guy sitting in the back of the class who looked like a TV star—an Italian MTV VJ, if you really want to know. Well, Francesco wasn't

"

You could say that Avocaderia was born on Instagram. We posted pics of everything avocado, and before we knew it, Avocaderia had gone viral before we'd even served one dish!

"

famous, but he did really know how to cook. Alessandro, on the other hand, was a self-proclaimed kitchen novice who could barely even peel an apple.

There was also our similar Italian upbringing to bring us together. We grew up like many Italians do—with a strong attachment to food and to family. We learned to cook by watching our grandmothers in the kitchen (we got playfully swatted with wooden spoons plenty of times for dipping our fingers in sauces!). We lived in the Italian countryside, where it was normal for us to spend two days each summer making two hundred pounds of tomato sauce to last our families an entire year. So it felt entirely natural for us to eventually transition into the business of food with Avocaderia.

Going to college was Francesco's first time away from home, and he liked having people over for dinner. He always had something to eat and drink in his apartment, even if that just meant simple snacks and Italian wine bought on the cheap. He liked feeling like he was building a family outside of his hometown of Prato. Francesco fed Alessandro, and in turn, Alessandro taught Francesco how to play poker and PlayStation (super-important skills in their own right). Of course, we played lots of soccer, too, which is how our dude friendship was solidified.

You could say that Avocaderia was born on Instagram. Before we opened our first location, we put up a basic website and created an Instagram account to see if people would be interested in the concept. We posted pics of everything avocado, and before we knew it, we were an overnight sensation—Avocaderia had gone viral before we'd served even one dish!

That summer, we got our first piece of press from *Eat Out*, a South African restaurant guide—and we didn't even have a location yet. The headline? "The world will soon have its first avocado bar and it sounds like heaven on earth." We knew finding the perfect spot was the next step, and getting situated at Industry City took us about a year. It was a lot of contract work and waiting and then go, go, go. Once the deal was sealed we rushed around like madmen for two weeks to get the design just right. We put up custom-made tiles, hung our now famous "Smashed in NYC" neon sign, picked the perfect plants to nestle by the register. A lot of thinking went into our design even if we were executing in a hurry—we knew the design would be as important to deliver on as the food, because we were creating not just a restaurant but an entire experience. Oh yeah, and then there was an entire menu to build.

That's where Alberto Gramigni, Francesco's cousin and a chef, came in. Francesco kept telling Alessandro how Alberto had a knack for making simple foods special—food you haven't seen a million times. We knew we didn't want Avocaderia to be a Mexican restaurant, but rather an avocado bar with a unique, bold perspective where flavor always comes first.

Alberto was fifteen years old when he first tasted an avocado—the first one among us to try one, actually. He was on vacation in Tulum, Mexico, with his family and they ordered guacamole—a game changer for him that got him rethinking everything he already knew about food. He could never have predicted at the time, but that trip would have a big impact on his life. Now, at Avocaderia, it's avocados all the time.

As Italians, we definitely could never have imagined that we would be serving dishes created around avocados for a living.

Until recently, you couldn't really even find avocados in Italy. But we always envisioned we'd start a movement, creating a tight-knit community where people could work on building healthier bodies and minds. We knew that making a difference in the world far beyond making a profit was our goal. We also became the first in the world to have an entire menu built on avocados—way beyond toast. From breakfast to dessert, avocado is the star ingredient in toasts, salads, grain bowls, burgers, soups, sandwiches, smoothies, and sweets.

The food at Avocaderia is playful—and packed with influences and ingredients from kitchens around the world, like those from Mexico, Morocco, China, Japan, Greece, and, of course, Italy. Alberto crisscrossed international cuisines, flavors, and textures with tradition and a lot of imagination to develop Avocaderia's own food style. That's why you'll find cool ingredients like shichimi togarashi from Japan sprinkled on our toasts; why you'll see dukkah from Egypt mixed into our salads; and why you'll taste za'atar from Lebanon in our bowls.

These days, thousands of people come to us from countries around the world, including faraway places like Australia and China. They land in New York City, hop off the plane, and come straight to Avocaderia. We could never have dreamed of such dedicated Avocaderia fans—truly humbling to say the least—or that there'd be so many Avocaderia locations in the works. Oh, and this cookbook? It's here to help you get the complete Avocaderia experience. If you're holding it in your hands, know that whether you live down the street from Avocaderia or across the country, you have Avocaderia's *corazón*, along with our bestselling recipes, essential kitchen tools, pantry of favorite ingredients, and everything you'd ever need to know about avocados. Get ready to make some incredible dishes and, if you're willing, reset your perspective on how delicious healthy eating can truly be.

"

While we may be introducing you to new flavors and ideas, everything on our menu is approachable and unpretentious. Guac with pita chips, anyone?

"

avo 101

———

WE'VE REACHED AVO-MANIA—and Avocaderia is no exception. Avocado consumption in America has tripled in the past decade and shows no signs of slowing down anytime soon. The USDA reported that Americans consumed 7.1 pounds of avocados in 2016, filling our shopping carts with what the Hass Avocado Board says amounts to $1.6 billion dollars' worth of avocados annually. If you're an avo lover like us, you should get in the know on your favorite fruit. Here's our cheat sheet:

what are avocados?

The avocado, botanically speaking, is a single-seeded berry, which grows on the *Persea americana*, aka the avocado tree. While this flowering tree is native to south central Mexico, it now grows in tropical climates globally. This good-for-you fruit comes in various sizes and shapes, including pear-shaped and egg-shaped varieties. Avocados have a glossy, pebbled skin that ranges in color from green to green-black to purple. Its flesh is soft, creamy, and pale green, with a large seed in the center.

At Avocaderia, we use Mexican Hass. We believe in sustainable avocado production and ethical trade practices, which encourage and support farmers while protecting the environment. Depending on where you live, it's likely your local grocery store imports them from any number of sources, and you might see different varieties in different seasons.

Our Top Avocado Varieties

HASS

At Avocaderia, we favor this creamy, nutty avocado, which makes up 95 percent of the market. Unless otherwise specified in the recipe, the avocados called for in this cookbook are medium size, weighing about 8 ounces and yielding 1 cup of avocado flesh.

SHAPE: oval

SIZE: 5 to 12 ounces

SEASON: in Michoacán, Mexico, from August to April; in California from April to September

DISTINGUISHING FEATURE: skin color changes during ripening from green to purplish-black

PINKERTON

This avocado can be even fuller in flavor than Hass avocados. It has a shorter growing season, so be on the lookout for Pinkertons in the spring.

SHAPE: pear

SIZE: 8 to 18 ounces

SEASON: spring

DISTINGUISHING FEATURE: small seed with super-creamy, pale green flesh

FUERTE

This variety is similar in size and shape to Hass avocados, but they are at their peak in the fall.

SHAPE: pear

SIZE: 5 to 14 ounces

SEASON: late fall through spring

DISTINGUISHING FEATURE: smooth, thin green skin

REED

This creamy, environmentally friendly variety requires less water to grow and produces more fruit than the Hass avocado.

SHAPE: round

SIZE: 8 to 18 ounces

SEASON: summer and early fall

DISTINGUISHING FEATURE: thick green skin with slight pebbling

ZUTANO

This pale green–fleshed avocado has an almost lemony flavor and light, silky texture as a result of its lower fat content.

SHAPE: pear

SIZE: 6 to 14 ounces

SEASON: September through early winter

DISTINGUISHING FEATURE: shiny, yellow-green skin

how to buy avocados

Avocados ripen off the tree, so buy them a little unripe and firm to the touch unless you plan to eat them the same day. Check ripeness by touch: Press down slightly on the stem—there should be slight resistance—and if the stem comes off, the avocado is overripe. Another method is to gently squeeze an avocado and see if there's a bit of give without being mushy. A ready-to-eat avocado will be nearly all black rather than green, and it'll have a slightly sweet smell—an underripe avo won't have any smell at all. Want perfect avos every day of the week? Buy them at different stages of ripeness: ripe and soft for today or tomorrow, and green and firm for the rest of the week.

how to store and ripen avocados

Store whole avocados at room temperature if they still need ripening or refrigerate them if you need to slow their ripening. Want to speed up the process? Ripe bananas are your answer. Just lay the bananas next to unripe avocados in a warm environment and your unripe avo worries will drift away. In even more of a rush? Wrap banana and avocado together in a sheet of newspaper or place them in a paper bag, which traps the ethylene gas released by the fruit, resulting in faster ripening.

HOW TO: Cut and Pit an Avocado

Halved, quartered, cubed, sliced, or mashed, cutting avocados can be tricky. And, yes, "avocado hand," or cutting yourself when halving an avocado, is real, but totally preventable. Start by placing the avocado on a clean cutting board. Then, using a small sharp knife, slice from skin to pit all the way around the avocado (1) and twist to open (2, 3). Sink the bottom part of the knife's blade into the pit (4) and twist to remove (5). Not knife savvy? Gently squeeze the avocado half containing the pit until the pit pops out, or use the tip of a spoon to push the side of the pit out. To get the most out of your avo, gently peel off the skin with your fingers (6) instead of scooping out the fruit with a spoon.

how to prevent browning

Once you cut into an avocado, you can reduce oxidation, or browning, by brushing the avocado flesh with olive oil or squeezing over
some lime or lemon juice, then directly covering the surface with
plastic wrap. Leaving the pit in can also reduce browning.

health benefits

The avo is the OG nutrient-dense superfood in the produce aisle—
and the reason healthy fat is our friend again. This wellness-savvy
staple is a prime source of fiber, antioxidants, and good fats, which
help lower cholesterol and boost metabolism. Avocados can also
help reduce inflammation, improve heart health, and regulate blood
sugar levels. Little-known fact: You'll get the most nutrients if you
peel off the skin rather than scooping out the flesh. You know that
dark green flesh directly under the skin? It contains the highest
concentration of antioxidants. Maybe the most eyebrow-raising
health benefit is that this fruit is said to rev up your libido. After
all, the word *avocado* is derived from the Aztec word for "testicle,"
ahuacatl, because the fruit is said to possess—you guessed it—aph-
rodisiac qualities. You be the judge.

Want to moisturize and detoxify your skin? You can actually use
avocado to make your own DIY face mask. Go ahead and slather
that green stuff on your skin! We do (how else do you think we stay
so beautiful?). See our recipe for Chilled Cucumber Soup (page
91), which doubles as a mask.

how to grow your own avocado tree

If you're ready to take your avo obsession to the next level, try growing your own avocado tree! Sure, it'll take a minimum of three years before your avo plant bears fruit—if ever. But it will look beautiful and add some green to your space.

1. Remove the avocado pit, rinse, and dry well.

2. Push up to four toothpicks into the pit at its widest part and suspend it over a glass of water with the pointy end sticking up. The water should cover about 1 inch of the pit.

3. Place in a warm spot and maintain the water level.

4. After anywhere from 2 to 6 weeks, you'll see roots and a stem sprout from the pit. When the stem is about 6 inches long, cut off the top half.

5. When the stem leafs again, transplant the seedling to a pot filled with loose, sandy soil. Plant the seedling root down, leaving the top half of the pit sticking out of the soil.

6. Keep the plant in a sunny place and water it frequently and lightly.

7. Pinch back the newest top leaves every time the stems grow another 6 inches to encourage growth.

"

Want a houseplant-turned-conversation starter? Get yourself an avocado tree!

"

kitchen essentials

WE RECOMMEND KEEPING your kitchen stocked with some base ingredients and tools so you'll always be prepared. (Trust us, you don't want to have to run to the grocery store in the middle of making a recipe! We've been there and we don't recommend it. Learn from our mistakes, people.) Don't worry, though, you probably already have a bunch of these on hand.

kitchen tools

- ☐ Small paring knife: to make avo roses
- ☐ Kitchen tongs: to layer ingredients on top of toast
- ☐ Flat metal spatula: to lift sliced avocados or avo roses, and to top toasts with spreads and dressings
- ☐ Silicone spatula: to scrape your bowl clean
- ☐ Potato masher: to prepare large amounts of guac for a big party

- ☐ Japanese mandoline: to cut thin slices of vegetables
- ☐ Microplane grater: to finely grate citrus zest
- ☐ High-speed blender: to make the smoothest, creamiest dressings and smoothies, fast
- ☐ Immersion blender: to blend soups and single-serve smoothies or dressings

- ☐ Plastic squeeze bottles: to drizzle over dressings and sauces, and as a storage container to use later
- ☐ Rice cooker: to cook various grains and keep them warm for serving
- ☐ Measuring cups and spoons: to accurately measure ingredients

pantry

SPICES

- [ ] Chiles (Aleppo pepper, dried chipotle pepper, canned chipotle peppers in adobo sauce)
  When combined with creamy avocado, the heat of the chiles helps balance the fattiness of the fruit.
- [ ] Sweet smoked paprika
- [ ] Shichimi togarashi (see note, page 129)
- [ ] Za'atar (see note, page 56)
- [ ] Ras el hanout (see note, page 178)
- [ ] Dukkah (see note, page 178)
- [ ] Turmeric

SEEDS & CEREALS

- [ ] Sesame seeds
- [ ] Tahini
- [ ] Spiced Seeds (page 178)
- [ ] Quinoa
- [ ] Puffed quinoa
  Exposing quinoa to a burst of heat makes this grain puffy, crispy, and nutty—ideal for sprinkling over salads or stirring into a granola for extra crunch.
- [ ] Farro

- [ ] Avo-Coconut Granola (page 180)

NUTS & DRIED FRUIT

- [ ] Cashews
- [ ] Almonds
- [ ] Pistachios
- [ ] Pecans
- [ ] Dates
- [ ] Coconut flakes (unsweetened)

TEAS

- [ ] Earl Grey
- [ ] Hibiscus flowers (see note, page 166)
- [ ] Matcha green tea (see note, page 154)

HERBS

- [ ] Dried Greek oregano
- [ ] Fresh basil
- [ ] Fresh mint
- [ ] Fresh rosemary, sage, and thyme
  This Mediterranean herb combo, rich in essential oils, boosts the flavor in recipes, allowing you to add less salt.

OIL

- [ ] Coconut oil
- [ ] Avocado oil
- [ ] Extra-virgin olive oil

As Italians, extra-virgin olive oil is our go-to oil for almost every dish. The floral, spicy notes of a good-quality olive oil pair well with our beloved avocado.

- [ ] Canola oil

SUGAR

- [ ] Agave syrup
- [ ] Brown sugar

DAIRY-FREE MILK

- [ ] Unsweetened almond milk
- [ ] Unsweetened soy milk
- [ ] Canned full-fat coconut milk
- [ ] Unsweetened cashew milk

EXTRAS

- [ ] Maldon sea salt
- [ ] Bread
- [ ] Panko bread crumbs
- [ ] Nutritional yeast (see note, page 179)
- [ ] Xanthan gum (see note, page 190)
- [ ] Kalamata olives
- [ ] Capers
- [ ] Green peppercorns in brine

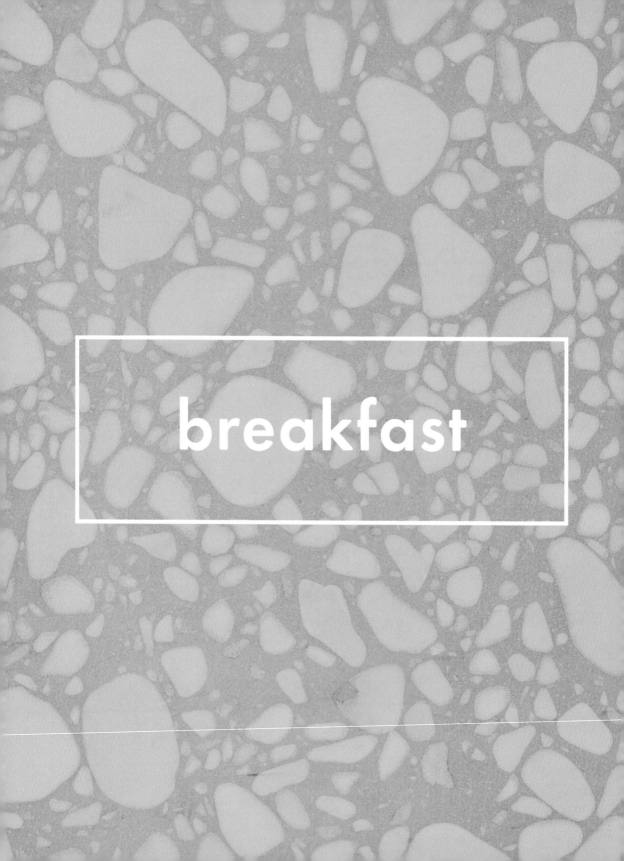

breakfast

Avo Pancakes with Blueberries
& Ginger Syrup   28

Baked Avo with Eggs &
Crunchy Ham   31

Avo Breakfast Bowl with Poached
Eggs & Hollandaise   32

Upside-Down Avo-Banana Cake
with Coconut Caramel   36

Nut Butter, Avo & Jelly Sandwich   39

Chill Out Toast   40

Avo-Yogurt Mousse with Granola   43

avo pancakes

with blueberries & ginger syrup

We're the first to admit that our avo pancakes are indulgent. Believe us, you'll want to pour over extra rum syrup, too. We made sure to balance things out with anti-inflammatory and antioxidant superpowers—the nutrient dream team of avo, blueberries, and ginger—that will help keep your skin clear and reduce bad cholesterol. Want perfectly round pancakes? Transfer the pancake batter to a plastic squeeze bottle and, as we say in Italy, *ecco*—or here you go!

SERVES 4

FOR THE GINGER SYRUP

¼ cup aged rum
¼ cup packed dark brown sugar
¼ cup granulated sugar
¼ teaspoon ground allspice
1 tablespoon finely grated fresh ginger

FOR THE PANCAKES

1 avocado, pitted and peeled
⅔ cup canned unsweetened full-fat coconut milk
1 cup all-purpose flour
¼ cup granulated sugar
1 teaspoon baking powder
½ teaspoon salt
2 large eggs
Canola oil, for greasing
Fresh blueberries, for topping and serving

1. **MAKE THE GINGER SYRUP:** In a medium saucepan, combine the rum, brown sugar, granulated sugar, allspice, and ¼ cup water and bring to a boil over medium heat. Reduce the heat and simmer, stirring occasionally, until the sugar has dissolved, about 3 minutes. Raise the heat to medium-high and add the ginger. Cook until slightly reduced, about 1 minute. Remove from the heat but keep warm.

2. **MAKE THE PANCAKES:** In a blender, combine the avocado and coconut milk and blend until smooth. Add the flour, granulated sugar, baking powder, salt, and eggs; blend on high speed until just combined. Refrigerate (still in the blender jar, with the lid on) for about 30 minutes.

3. Heat a large nonstick skillet over medium heat and grease it lightly with oil. Scoop ¼-cup portions of the batter onto the skillet and spread to form 3-inch rounds. Top each with some blueberries and cook, flipping once, until the pancakes are golden, about 2 minutes on each side. Transfer to a plate and repeat with the remaining batter, adding more oil to the skillet between batches as necessary.

4. Serve the pancakes topped with the warm ginger syrup and more blueberries.

baked avo
with eggs & crunchy ham

This recipe is a real game changer for protein lovers. And bonus: It comes in an adorable avocado boat! What's not to love?! Being Italian, we're partial to prosciutto, but go ahead and experiment with other dry-cured meats, like spicy chorizo or pepperoni. Just before baking, we freeze the avocado so it doesn't get overcooked.

SERVES 2

1 avocado, halved and pitted
2 large eggs, separated
2 tablespoons grated Parmesan cheese, plus more for sprinkling
Salt and black pepper
Olive oil, for drizzling
6 thin slices prosciutto
Ciabatta, cut into slices, for serving

1. Preheat the oven to 425°F.

2. Using a spoon and working with one avocado half at a time, scoop out about 2 tablespoons avocado to form a larger hole where the pit was; freeze the avocado halves for about 20 minutes.

3. In a small bowl, whisk together the egg whites, Parmesan, and a generous pinch of salt. Place the frozen avocado halves on a baking sheet; fill each pit hole with half the egg white mixture and 1 egg yolk. Sprinkle with Parmesan and drizzle all over with olive oil. Place the prosciutto slices and bread strips on the baking sheet alongside the avocado; bake until the prosciutto and bread are crisp, about 6 minutes, then transfer them to a plate. Continue to bake the avocados until the egg whites are set but the yolks are still runny, about 15 minutes more.

4. Divide the baked avocado halves, prosciutto, and bread between two plates and sprinkle with a pinch of pepper.

avo
breakfast
bowl
with poached eggs & hollandaise

You know those nights when you stare into the fridge wondering what to eat? This impossibly simple to make breakfast-for-dinner bowl is your answer. We lightened up eggs Benedict by swapping in avocado for English muffins and a low-maintenance hollandaise for the classic egg-based version. If you don't have a squeeze bottle to use for the hollandaise sauce, just place it in a resealable plastic bag and cut a tiny corner off when you're ready to use it.

SERVES 2

FOR THE HOLLANDAISE

¼ cup plus 2 tablespoons cream cheese, at room temperature

¼ cup plus 2 tablespoons warm water

2 tablespoons canola oil

½ teaspoon ground turmeric

½ teaspoon salt

FOR THE BREAKFAST BOWL

2 slices smoked ham

¼ cup mashed avocado

1 tablespoon Lime Citronette dressing (page 190)

1 avocado, halved, pitted, thinly sliced, and shaped into a rose (see page 34)

2 large eggs, poached (see at right)

½ teaspoon sweet smoked paprika

1. **MAKE THE HOLLANDAISE:** In a small bowl, mix together the cream cheese, warm water, canola oil, turmeric, and salt until combined; transfer to a squeeze bottle and keep warm in a heatproof bowl of water set over a saucepan of simmering water.

2. **MAKE THE BREAKFAST BOWL:** Place the ham on a microwave-safe plate and microwave on high until crispy, about 2 minutes; break into small pieces.

3. Mix the mashed avocado and the dressing and divide between two small bowls. Top each with an avocado rose and a poached egg. Place the crispy ham alongside each rose, drizzle with hollandaise sauce, and sprinkle with the paprika.

HOW TO: Poach an Egg

1. Fill a medium saucepan with a few inches of water and heat to a simmer.

2. Working with 1 egg at a time, crack each egg into a small bowl, lower to the surface of the water, and gently pour in the egg.

3. Simmer, undisturbed, to your desired doneness, about 3 minutes for a runny yolk or 5 minutes for a firm yolk.

4. Use a slotted spoon to gently transfer the egg to paper towels to drain.

HOW TO: Make an Avo Rose

Using a sharp paring knife, cut a ripe but firm avocado in half; remove the pit and peel the avocado. Cut each avocado half crosswise into super-thin, even slices (1). Gently fan out the avocado slices (2, 3), beginning at one end and twisting toward the center like a pinwheel (4, 5), shaping the avocado into a rose (6).

" Not feeling so rose-y? Don't sweat it—just thinly slice and serve instead. "

upside-down avo-banana cake

with coconut caramel

Avocado and banana were totally meant to be eaten together. Our unorthodox take on banana bread uses avocado and full-fat coconut milk instead of butter or shortening and reduces sugar by swapping in extra banana. The result? An incredibly moist cake perfect for an energizing breakfast or afternoon pick-me-up. We serve this cake upside down to reveal the drool-worthy caramelized bananas—super 'grammable.

MAKES ONE 6-INCH SQUARE CAKE

¼ cup plus 3 tablespoons packed brown sugar

¼ cup canned unsweetened full-fat coconut milk, plus more as needed

2 bananas, sliced lengthwise, plus ⅔ cup mashed ripe bananas

½ avocado, pitted and peeled

1 teaspoon fresh lemon juice

3 tablespoons coconut oil, melted

1 large egg

1 cup sifted cake flour

1½ teaspoons baking powder

½ teaspoon ground cinnamon

1. Preheat the oven to 375°F. Line the bottom of a 6-inch square baking pan with parchment paper.

2. In a small saucepan, combine 3 tablespoons of the brown sugar and 2 tablespoons water and heat over medium heat until the mixture starts to get syrupy and turns a deep golden brown. Stir in the coconut milk until combined, adding more as needed, 1 tablespoon at a time, until the mixture is thick but pourable. Pour into the prepared baking pan and top with the banana slices.

3. In a blender, combine the ⅔ cup mashed bananas, the avocado, and the lemon juice and blend until smooth.

4. In a medium bowl, whisk together the coconut oil, egg, remaining ¼ cup brown sugar, and the avocado mixture until smooth. Whisk in the flour, baking powder, and cinnamon. Pour the batter into the prepared baking pan over the sliced bananas and bake until golden, about 50 minutes. Let cool completely on a wire rack.

nut butter, avo & jelly sandwich

Coming from Italy, we didn't grow up on peanut butter and jelly sandwiches like most kids in America. That's probably why we're so fascinated by them—and by how good they can be if you give yourself creative license to think outside the lunch box. After all, we've come a long way since Wonder Bread, don't you think? We stack this sandwich four bread slices high to give each nut and fruit layer major props.

SERVES 2

1 avocado, pitted and peeled

1 tablespoon plus 1 teaspoon agave syrup

2 teaspoons fresh lemon juice

12 fresh raspberries

8 (¼-inch-thick) slices white or multigrain bread

¼ cup creamy nut butter, preferably peanut

¼ cup raspberry jam

1. In a blender, combine the avocado, agave, and lemon juice and blend until smooth.

2. Crush the raspberries in a small bowl.

3. Spread the avocado mixture over 2 of the bread slices.

4. Spread the peanut butter over 2 more bread slices.

5. Spread the jam over 2 other bread slices and top with the crushed raspberries.

6. To assemble, stack up the 3 slices with toppings and top with one of the remaining slices of bread. Trim the edges and cut each sandwich into 3 rectangles.

chill out toast

Our long-running joke at Avocaderia is that our cofounder Alessandro is a bad cook. Terrible. The worst. Put aside the fact that he has started many kitchen fires and you have this: Avocaderia would have never existed if not for one of Alessandro's rare attempts to feed himself. Years ago, before he moved to New York City, Ale crafted an early version of the Chill Out and was so inspired that he began dreaming up other ways to use avocado beyond toasts, and Avocaderia was born. The rest is delicious history.

SERVES 2

⅔ cup mashed avocado

2 tablespoons Lime Citronette dressing (page 190)

2 thick-cut slices multigrain bread, toasted

Maldon sea salt

Aleppo pepper flakes

Shichimi togarashi (see page 129)

1. In a small bowl, stir together the mashed avocado and dressing.

2. Top each toast slice with the mashed avocado mixture. Sprinkle with salt, Aleppo pepper, and shichimi togarashi.

VARIATION
Chill Out Toast with Egg

Halve 1 avocado, slice thinly, and shape each half into a rose (see page 34). Poach 2 eggs as described on page 32. After spreading each toast slice with the mashed avocado, top with an avocado rose and a poached egg, then sprinkle with the salt, Aleppo pepper, and shichimi togarashi.

avo-yogurt mousse
with granola

This mousse is so versatile. Here we pair it with our granola and some fresh fruit for breakfast, but you can scoop it on top of desserts or eat it on its own. You can even spoon it straight from the blender—we won't tell on you because we're guilty many times over!

SERVES 2

½ avocado, pitted and peeled

1 cup plain Greek yogurt

2 tablespoons agave syrup

2 teaspoons fresh lime juice

½ teaspoon finely grated lime zest

Avo-Coconut Granola (page 180), for topping

Fresh fruit of your choice, for topping (optional)

1. In a blender, combine the avocado, yogurt, agave, and lime juice and blend on high speed until smooth, about 20 seconds. Stir in the lime zest. Serve with granola and fruit, if desired.

toasts + sandwiches

el salmon

This is your next-level lox and cream cheese right here. Go ahead and layer on avocado, citrusy dressing, and our Green Pico, a crunchy combo of cucumber, celery, and jicama. This recipe was inspired by a Fourth of July trip to Montauk, New York, where Francesco and Alessandro made a version of this toast as a quick snack for friends. Everyone loved it so much, it was gone before Francesco and Alessandro could even snag a bite.

SERVES 2

2 thick-cut slices multigrain bread, toasted

¼ cup cream cheese

1 avocado, pitted, peeled, and thinly sliced

3 ounces smoked salmon

¼ cup Green Pico (page 186)

2 tablespoons Lime Citronette dressing (page 190)

Black sesame seeds, for sprinkling

1. Top each toast slice with the cream cheese, avocado, salmon, and pico; drizzle each with the dressing and sprinkle with sesame seeds.

mediterranean toast

This was the first toast Alberto developed, and it happens to be our team's favorite. It's also the toast that won the hearts of each and every shark during our appearance on ABC's *Shark Tank*. Who can resist tapenade layered with buttery avocado? For this one, we take classic Greek flavors like olives, tomatoes, and feta, then top them with a Middle Eastern pantry staple, *dukkah*—a bold, earthy nut-and-spice blend that gets its name from the Egyptian word for "to pound."

SERVES 2

2 thick-cut slices sourdough bread, toasted

¼ cup Olive Tapenade (page 185)

⅔ cup mashed avocado

6 cherry tomatoes, quartered

12 sun-dried tomatoes in olive oil, chopped

¼ cup crumbled feta cheese

Olive oil, for drizzling

Pistachio Dukkah (page 178), for sprinkling

1. Top each toast slice with the tapenade, avocado, cherry tomatoes, sun-dried tomatoes, and feta; drizzle with olive oil and sprinkle with dukkah.

let it beet

Our cofounder Alessandro came up with this punny name when we were tinkering with this toast in the test kitchen. Customers will sometimes even break out into song when they order the Let It Beet, which is one of our most popular toasts (and one of our most Instagrammed menu items because of its vibrant colors).

SERVES 2

2 thick-cut slices sourdough bread, toasted

⅓ cup Beet Hummus (page 184)

1 avocado, pitted, peeled, and thinly sliced

1 cup loosely packed arugula

A few thin slices watermelon radish (or other radish)

2 tablespoons Agave Mustard Dressing (page 191)

4 tablespoons Spiced Seeds (page 178)

1. Top each toast slice with the hummus, avocado, arugula, and radish; drizzle with the mustard and sprinkle with the seeds.

avo tuna tostadas

Francesco spent several years in Mexico City, and a lot happened in that time: he fell in love (with a girl) and then fell in love again (with avocado). So when *Good Day New York* asked us to demo a dish on live TV for Cinco de Mayo, Francesco brilliantly came up with this tostada, using tuna instead of the typical beef or chicken to keep it lighter. The hibiscus water marinade mellows the tuna just a bit while the Lime Citronette dressing keeps the dish bright. Our Earl Grey–Hibiscus Iced Tea (page 166) pairs perfectly here.

SERVES 2

FOR THE TUNA

¼ cup hibiscus water (see below)

¼ cup low-sodium soy sauce

4 ounces sushi-grade tuna, cut into ¾-inch cubes (about ½ cup)

FOR THE TOSTADAS

½ cup mashed avocado, plus ½ avocado, pitted, peeled, and cubed

2 tablespoons Lime Citronette dressing (page 190)

2 store-bought tostada shells

2 tablespoons Green Pico (page 186)

1 teaspoon Maldon sea salt

2 teaspoons black sesame seeds

TIP:

Hibiscus is full of amazing health benefits: It can help treat high blood pressure and high cholesterol, and could also help speed up your metabolism.

1. **MARINATE THE TUNA:** In a small bowl, whisk together the hibiscus water and soy sauce. Submerge the tuna in the mixture and let marinate for 5 minutes; drain and pat dry.

2. **MAKE THE TOSTADAS:** In a small bowl, stir together the mashed avocado and dressing.

3. Spread the mashed avocado mixture over the tostada shells. Top with the avocado cubes, marinated tuna, and pico; sprinkle each with the sea salt and sesame seeds.

HOW TO: Make Hibiscus Water

1. Combine equal parts dried hibiscus flowers and hot water.

2. Let steep overnight or for at least 3 hours.

3. Strain the hibiscus water through a fine-mesh sieve into a storage container; discard the flowers. Store refrigerated in an airtight container for up to 1 week.

El Salmon
(page 46)

Mediterranean
Toast
(page 49)

za'atar & lemon toast

Za'atar gets its name and vibrant green color from the spice blend's main ingredient, dried wild thyme leaves (*za'atar* means "thyme" in Arabic). You can find za'atar at your local spice shop or online (see Resources, page 198). You've gotta try za'atar on pita—it's a classic for a reason—but we highly encourage experimenting. Sprinkle it on dips like hummus or tzatziki, roasted vegetables, and way more. We'll let you thank us later.

SERVES 2

⅔ cup mashed avocado, plus 6 thin slices avocado (about 2 avocados total)

2 teaspoons Lime Citronette dressing (page 190)

2 pitas, store-bought or homemade (page 116), brushed with olive oil and toasted

1 teaspoon za'atar

½ teaspoon lemon zest

2 tablespoons Pecan Chermoula (page 187), for serving

1. In a small bowl, stir together the mashed avocado and dressing. Top each pita with the mashed avocado mixture and the avocado slices. Sprinkle with the za'atar and lemon zest, and serve with the chermoula.

back to the roots

Admit it: Come October, everyone's jonesing for sweater weather and craving anything squash-worthy. This toast—smothered with roasted kabocha squash and topped with peppery greens and crunchy Spiced Seeds—has that autumn appeal. Didn't think it could get any better than this? It also pairs perfectly with a pumpkin spice latte or your favorite "golden milk." Don't worry—we'll never call you basic.

SERVES 2

2 thick-cut slices sourdough bread, toasted

⅔ cup mashed roasted kabocha squash (see at right)

1 avocado, pitted, peeled, and thinly sliced

2 cups lightly packed spicy greens, such as arugula, watercress, mustard greens, and/or mizuna

Vegan Chipotle & Turmeric Mayo (page 195), for drizzling

Spiced Seeds (page 178), for sprinkling

1. Top each toast slice with the squash, avocado, and greens. Drizzle with mayo and sprinkle with seeds.

HOW TO: Roast Squash

1. Preheat the oven to 400°F. Line a baking sheet with parchment paper.

2. Halve and seed the squash. Place the halves cut-side up on the prepared baking sheet.

3. Drizzle generously with olive oil and season with salt.

4. Roast until fork-tender, about 50 minutes. Let cool, then scoop the squash flesh into a small bowl and mash.

green peas, mint & burrata toast

This is our riff on a beloved Italian springtime bruschetta. If you can't find the softer burrata, swap in its cousin, mozzarella, but don't skimp on the fresh mint—it pulls together the whole dish. Just be careful when taking a bite—the burrata is deliciously messy.

SERVES 2

FOR THE PEA SPREAD

2 sprigs fresh mint
2 cloves garlic
1 tablespoon plus
    1 teaspoon olive oil
2 cups frozen peas
½ teaspoon sugar
½ teaspoon salt
Black pepper

FOR THE TOAST

1 piece ciabatta bread
    (about 5 inches square
    each), split and toasted
1 avocado, pitted, peeled,
    and sliced
2 small balls burrata
    cheese, at room
    temperature
Small fresh mint leaves, for
    topping
Pea shoots, for topping
    (optional)
Olive oil, for drizzling
Black pepper, for sprinkling

1. **MAKE THE PEA SPREAD:** In a small saucepan, combine the mint, garlic, and oil and cook over low heat for 30 seconds. Stir in the peas, sugar, salt, and pepper; cook for 5 minutes. Add ¼ cup water and cover; cook until the peas are fork-tender and there's still some liquid in the pan, about 10 minutes. Remove from the heat. Reserve 1 tablespoon of the whole peas for topping the toasts. Transfer the remaining pea mixture to a food processor and pulse until coarsely mashed.

2. **MAKE THE TOAST:** Spread about ⅓ cup pea spread over each toasted ciabatta bottom. Divide the sliced avocado between the toasts, placing it in the center, and set the burrata on top. Scatter over the reserved cooked peas, mint, and pea shoots (if using), then drizzle with olive oil and sprinkle with pepper.

avo chicken club

We don't believe that Caesar dressing is just for salads, so we went ahead and slathered it onto some slightly sweet, earthy pumpernickel bread and smashed avo. Topped with spicy greens in addition to traditional romaine, this Avo Club will sneakily light up your brain's pleasure centers and give you your vitamin and nutrient fix. The only way to improve on this masterpiece is to add some protein—we recommend roasted chicken here, but feel free to make it vegetarian with baked tofu (see below).

SERVES 2

½ cup mashed avocado

4 slices pumpernickel bread, toasted

⅔ cup sliced or shredded roasted chicken (homemade or store-bought)

4 romaine leaves, halved crosswise

2 cups lightly packed spicy greens, such as arugula, watercress, mustard greens, and/or mizuna

2 tablespoons Vegan Avo Caesar Dressing (page 193)

1. Spread the avocado on 2 bread slices. Top the other 2 slices with the chicken, romaine, spicy greens, and dressing, then sandwich together.

HOW TO: Bake Tofu

1. Preheat the oven to 400°F. Line a baking sheet with parchment paper.

2. Cut 1 (10-ounce) block firm tofu into ¾-inch cubes and put them in a bowl.

3. Drizzle the tofu with 1 tablespoon light soy sauce and 2 teaspoons toasted sesame oil. Spread the tofu cubes over the prepared baking sheet.

4. Bake for 8 to 10 minutes, until golden. Let cool slightly before serving.

mozzarella & avo pesto melt

We broke all the conventional grilled cheese rules—no white bread, butter, or American cheese here—and we're never going back. Instead, thick-cut multigrain bread sandwiches mozzarella cheese, avocado, kale, and pesto to make the ultimate creamy, herby cheese melt. If you're in the mood to switch things up, swap in chipotle mayo (page 195) for the pesto and arugula for the kale.

SERVES 2

4 slices multigrain bread

4 (¼-inch-thick) slices mozzarella cheese

¼ cup Traditional Guac (page 125)

¼ cup Avo Pesto (page 104)

1 cup finely chopped kale leaves

1. Top 2 slices of the bread with 1 cheese slice each. Spread the guac and pesto over the cheese; top with the kale, remaining cheese slices, and a slice of bread.

2. Heat a panini press. Toast the sandwiches until the bread is golden and the cheese has melted, about 4 minutes.

salads +
bowls

quinoa & friends

This warm, satisfying grain bowl is a cult classic and one of our most versatile dishes—quinoa and avocado go with just about anything. When we named this dish, we thought that if we kept the base consistent, we could rotate seasonal fruits and veggies into the recipe, which is where we got the idea for "& Friends." Think raw veggies in the warmer months and cooked, heartier veggies in the colder months.

SERVES 4

2 teaspoons canola oil

1 cup ½-inch asparagus pieces

2 cups cooked quinoa, kept warm (preferably in a rice cooker)

2 cups loosely packed curly kale leaves, torn into bite-size pieces

1 cup mashed avocado, plus 2 avocados, pitted, peeled, and sliced

1 cup thinly sliced celery, plus celery leaves for topping

1 cup thinly sliced fennel

¼ cup Lime Citronette dressing (page 190)

½ cup puffed quinoa, for topping

TIP:

Fennel is usually available year-round, but it's best eaten in its peak season from late fall through early spring. It has a slightly sweet, anise-like flavor and tastes super refreshing when eaten raw. Fennel is one of our favorite superfoods, as it can help prevent anemia and regulate blood pressure.

1. In a skillet, heat the oil over high heat. Add the asparagus and cook, tossing occasionally, until slightly charred and still crunchy, about 5 minutes.

2. In a medium bowl, stir together the quinoa, kale, and mashed avocado; transfer to a serving bowl. Top with the celery, celery leaves, fennel, charred asparagus, and sliced avocados. Drizzle with the dressing and top with the puffed quinoa.

> **HOW TO: Cook Quinoa**
>
> In a medium saucepan, combine 1 cup rinsed quinoa with 2 cups water and bring to a boil. Cover, reduce the heat to low, and simmer until tender, about 15 minutes.

greek island salad

Alberto is constantly on the hunt for international flavors, and he takes careful notes on every meal he has when he's traveling (what a life, right?!). He went to Athens one summer to visit a friend and ate his weight in Greek food, from moussaka to souvlaki to gyro. Without fail, Greek salads were served at each meal. This is Alberto's version—with a healthy dose of avo added, of course. If you want to incorporate more traditional Greek flavors here, replace the Yogurt & Fresh Herbs dressing with a little olive oil, red wine vinegar, salt, and dried oregano.

SERVES 4

4 cups loosely packed mixed salad greens

2 cups halved cherry tomatoes

2 cups diced cucumbers

½ cup pitted Kalamata olives, halved lengthwise

½ cup sun-dried tomatoes in olive oil, chopped

½ cup Yogurt & Fresh Herbs dressing (page 185)

2 avocados, pitted, peeled, and sliced into wedges

½ cup crumbled feta cheese

½ cup Pistachio Dukkah (page 178)

1. Place the greens in a serving bowl and top with the cherry tomatoes, cucumbers, olives, and sun-dried tomatoes. Drizzle with the dressing and add the avocado wedges, feta, and dukkah.

super greens

When we moved to New York, we found it difficult to find a simple, balanced salad like this one—more often than not, delis here load up on unhealthy extras, drown the salad in dressing, and skimp on the lettuce. Our Super Greens remedies that so you're getting a salad that tastes good and is actually good for you. Oh, and because we love carbs as much as the next Italian, we couldn't resist adding some croutons for just a little bit of crunch.

SERVES 4

2 teaspoons canola oil

1 cup ½-inch asparagus pieces

8 cups loosely packed mixed salad greens

4 cups loosely packed curly kale leaves, torn into bite-size pieces

½ cup Lime Citronette dressing (page 190)

1 cup thinly sliced celery

1 cup thinly sliced fennel

2 avocados, pitted, peeled, and cubed

½ cup Croutons (page 179)

1. In a skillet, heat the oil over high heat. Add the asparagus, tossing occasionally, until slightly charred and still crunchy, about 5 minutes.

2. Place the greens and kale in a serving bowl and toss with ½ cup of the dressing. Top with the celery, fennel, charred asparagus, and avocados. Drizzle with the remaining ¼ cup dressing and top with the croutons.

Beets & Blue
(page 74)

Quinoa & Friends
(page 67)

Super Greens
(page 71)

beets & blue

Fact: Blue cheese is delicious. If you're wary of it, consider giving Ol' Blue another try here. The earthy beets tone down the pungency just a bit, so this is a great way to ease yourself into stinkier varieties of cheese. We also like pairing this salad with a balancing drink like Ginger-Mint Lemonade (page 168).

SERVES 4

8 cups loosely packed arugula

2 cups diced cooked beets (see below)

½ watermelon radish (or other radish), thinly sliced

1 cup crumbled blue cheese

½ cup Agave Mustard Dressing (page 191)

2 avocados, pitted, peeled, and cubed

½ cup Spiced Seeds (page 178)

1. Place the arugula in a serving bowl and top with the beets, radishes, and blue cheese. Drizzle with the dressing and top with the avocados and seeds.

HOW TO: Cook Beets

Bring a pot of salted water to a boil. Add the beets and cook until tender, about 1½ hours. Drain the beets. Peel the beets and cut into 1-inch pieces; let cool.

TIP:

Adding some raw fennel to this dish complements the flavor of the beets *and* makes it even healthier.

avo-orange sicilian salad

When we think of Sicily, which is at the bottom of the boot that comprises the southern part of Italy, our minds go to sun-baked ruins like Taormina, the still-active volcano Mount Etna, and . . . oranges, in particular blood oranges, a prized crop in Sicily. This is our play on a classic Sicilian salad that offsets the fruit's tart sweetness with a savory dressing. Serve this during winter when you need a pick-me-up.

SERVES 4

½ cup raw almonds

2 teaspoons canola oil

2 teaspoons smoked sweet paprika

3 teaspoons salt

3 tablespoons olive oil

4 small blood oranges, segmented, cubed, and juice reserved

2 teaspoons Dijon mustard

1 teaspoon red wine vinegar

1 teaspoon dried oregano

1 teaspoon fennel seeds, crushed

½ teaspoon black pepper

4 cups loosely packed mixed salad greens with arugula

1 fennel bulb, thinly sliced and placed in an ice water bath

½ red onion, thinly sliced and placed in an ice water bath

8 radishes, thinly sliced and placed in an ice water bath

½ watermelon radish (or other radish), thinly sliced and placed in an ice water bath

2 avocados, pitted, peeled, and cubed

1 cup pitted green olives, halved

1. Preheat the oven to 350°F.

2. On a baking sheet, toss together the almonds, canola oil, paprika, and 1 teaspoon of the salt; toast until fragrant, about 15 minutes. Transfer to a paper towel–lined plate and let cool.

3. In a small bowl, whisk together the olive oil, reserved orange juice, mustard, vinegar, oregano, fennel seeds, pepper, and remaining 2 teaspoons salt.

4. Place the greens in a serving bowl and top with the fennel, onion, radishes, avocados, orange cubes, roasted almonds, and olives; drizzle with the dressing.

avo caesar

Caesars often get a bad rap because even though they masquerade as healthy, they're usually fattening and full of empty calories. But we love the flavors of a classic Caesar, so we decided to create a nutritious vegan version of the classic. Want to make this salad a complete meal? Top it with roasted chicken or baked tofu (see page 168).

SERVES 4

2 large heads romaine lettuce, leaves left whole

2 cups spicy greens, such as arugula, watercress, mustard greens, and/or mizuna

3 or 4 pitted and peeled avocado halves

½ cup Vegan Avo Caesar Dressing (page 193)

½ cup Croutons (page 179)

¼ cup Cashew Parmesan (page 179)

1. Place the romaine, spicy greens, and avocado halves on a serving platter. Drizzle with the dressing and top with the croutons and cashew parmesan.

watermelon salad

This was the first special Alberto created for our summer menu. True story: He locked himself in the test kitchen with a giant watermelon and didn't emerge until he had developed some great new dishes, including this salad's key ingredient—watermelon pickles—using watermelon rind, which usually just gets tossed in the trash.

SERVES 4

8 cups arugula

2 avocados, pitted and peeled

½ cup Raspberry Balsamic dressing (page 192)

6 ounces (1 cup) fresh watermelon cubes

½ cup Watermelon Pickles (see at right)

½ watermelon radish (or other radish), cut into matchsticks

½ cup cubed feta cheese

Puffed quinoa, for sprinkling

TIP:

Watermelon season runs throughout the summer all the way into September, making this salad the perfect party dish for every summer holiday. Include it in your Labor Day festivities to celebrate the few remaining days of our favorite flavor season.

1. Divide the arugula among four plates. Place an avocado half cut-side up on each and fill the cavity with 2 tablespoons of the dressing. Top with the watermelon cubes, watermelon pickles, radish, and feta. Sprinkle with puffed quinoa.

HOW TO: Make Watermelon Pickles

1. In a saucepan, combine 1 cup water, ½ cup apple cider vinegar, 3 tablespoons dried hibiscus flowers, 2 tablespoons sugar, and 1 tablespoon salt and bring to a boil over high heat. Stir until the sugar and salt have dissolved.

2. Meanwhile, cut about 1 cup's worth of the white part of the watermelon rinds into small (about ⅓-inch) cubes (discard the dark-green peel). Submerge them in the hot brine. Let cool to room temperature and then refrigerate in an airtight container for up to 2 weeks.

roasted roots farro bowl

While farro is a great source of protein and naturally high in fiber, its main health benefit is that it's said to counteract free-radical growth, which is responsible for aging and cellular degeneration. Translation? You're basically telling wrinkles to shove off by eating this. Magic.

SERVES 4

FOR THE ROASTED VEGETABLES

1 sweet potato, peeled and cut into ¾-inch cubes (1 cup)

1 small or ½ large winter squash, peeled and cut into ¾-inch cubes (1 cup)

2 medium carrots, cut into ¾-inch cubes (⅔ cup)

½ medium celery root (celeriac), peeled and cut into ¾-inch cubes (⅓ cup)

2 sprigs fresh sage

2 sprigs fresh thyme

2 sprigs fresh rosemary

2 teaspoons olive oil

1 teaspoon salt

FOR THE FARRO BOWL

4 cups cooked farro (see at right), kept warm

¼ cup Vegan Chipotle & Turmeric Mayo (page 195)

2 cups spicy greens, such as arugula, watercress, and/or mustard greens

2 avocados, pitted, peeled, and cubed

¼ cup Agave Mustard Dressing (page 191)

1 tablespoon hulled pumpkin seeds, toasted, for topping

1. **MAKE THE ROASTED VEGETABLES:** Preheat the oven to 400°F. Line a baking sheet with parchment paper.

2. In a large bowl, toss together the sweet potatoes, squash, carrots, celery root, sage, thyme, rosemary, olive oil, and salt. Transfer to the prepared baking sheet and cover with foil. Roast for 20 minutes, then remove the foil and roast until golden, about 20 minutes more.

3. **MAKE THE FARRO BOWL:** In a serving bowl, mix together the farro and mayo. Add the greens, roasted vegetables, and avocados. Drizzle with the dressing and top with the pumpkin seeds.

HOW TO: Cook Farro

Place 2 cups uncooked farro in a saucepan and add enough water to cover. Bring to a boil. Reduce the heat to medium, cover, and cook until just tender, about 12 minutes. Drain and transfer to a bowl.

Watermelon
Salad (page 79)

Greek Island
Salad
(page 68)

Avo Caesar
(page 76)

avo tabbouleh bowl

Middle Eastern ingredients like pomegranate, eggplant, pistachio, baharat spice mix, and Aleppo pepper star in this grain bowl. The secret to removing pomegranate seeds from the fruit? Cut the pomegranate in half, hold one half flesh-side down over a bowl, and smack it with a big wooden spoon. The seeds will fall right into the bowl.

SERVES 4

2½ cups bulgur

1 eggplant, cut into ⅓-inch cubes (2 cups)

Salt

1 teaspoon baharat spice blend (see Tip, below)

3 tablespoons olive oil

16 cherry tomatoes, halved

¼ cup thinly sliced celery

¼ cup thinly sliced fennel

3 tablespoons Tomato-Herb Dressing (page 194)

2 avocados, pitted, peeled, and cubed

¼ cup pomegranate seeds

¼ cup Pistachio Dukkah (page 178)

1. Preheat the oven to 425°F.

2. Bring a pot of salted water to a boil. Add the bulgur and cook until tender, about 8 minutes. Drain and rinse with cold water to cool completely.

3. Spread the eggplant on a baking sheet. Sprinkle with salt, the baharat spice blend, and 1 tablespoon of the olive oil. Roast until golden, about 15 minutes.

4. In a large bowl, toss together the bulgur, roasted eggplant, cherry tomatoes, celery, fennel, and dressing. Transfer to a serving bowl and top with the avocados, pomegranate seeds, and dukkah. Drizzle with the remaining 2 tablespoons olive oil.

TIP:

Baharat is a Middle Eastern smoky-sweet, all-purpose spice blend, which varies greatly country to country and even home to home. Often the blend contains coriander, cinnamon, cloves, allspice, cumin, cardamom, nutmeg, and black pepper.

portobello road bowl

We came up with this dish during the doldrums of winter. After probably, oh, the twelfth time that snow had been dumped all over New York City, we were looking to create a veg-filled dish that would tide us over until spring and the bounty of produce that would be available to us. We packed this bowl full of nourishment by adding kale and hummus, so eat this on colder days when you're feeling peaky, and we guarantee you'll feel better!

SERVES 4

8 ounces firm tofu, cut into ½-inch cubes (1 cup)

Olive oil

3 portobello mushrooms

Salt and black pepper

3 cups cooked brown rice (see page 87), still warm

2 cups loosely packed kale leaves

1 cup chickpea hummus (see page 184)

¼ cup warm water

2 avocados, pitted, peeled, and sliced

⅔ cup Vegan Chipotle & Turmeric Mayo (page 195)

½ cup Cashew Parmesan (page 179), for topping

1. Preheat the oven to 400°F.

2. In a medium bowl, toss the tofu with a little oil to coat and spread in an even layer on a baking sheet. Put the mushrooms on a separate baking sheet and brush with oil. Sprinkle the tofu and mushrooms with salt and pepper. Roast the tofu until golden, 8 to 10 minutes, and the mushroom until browned, about 15 minutes. Let the mushroom cool slightly and then cut into ½-inch cubes (you should have about 1 cup).

3. In a medium bowl, stir together the brown rice, kale, hummus, and warm water until smooth and creamy. Transfer to a serving bowl and top with the tofu, mushrooms, and avocado slices. Drizzle with the mayo and top with the parmesan.

salmon, seaweed & avo poke bowl

with ginger-sesame dressing

Poke bowls seemingly popped up out of nowhere at fast-casual places in Los Angeles and then quickly spread across the country at trendy eateries like Sweetfin and Poke-Poke. But poke—very fresh raw fish, seasoned simply—actually originated in Hawaii hundreds of years ago and is still considered a staple there. Basic poke consists of raw fish with soy sauce and sesame oil, but we've rounded ours out to a fully satisfying meal.

SERVES 4

FOR THE GINGER-SESAME DRESSING

- 1 tablespoon plus ½ teaspoon rice wine vinegar
- 1 tablespoon tahini
- 2 teaspoons toasted sesame oil
- 2 teaspoons sriracha
- 2 teaspoons dark soy sauce
- 1 teaspoon sugar or agave syrup
- ½ teaspoon salt
- 1 tablespoon grated fresh ginger
- 3 tablespoons canola oil

FOR THE POKE BOWL

- 4 cups cooked brown rice (see opposite page)
- 1½ cups sushi-grade raw salmon, diced into ½-inch cubes
- 1 cup frozen shelled edamame
- ⅓ cup (about 1 small) julienned watermelon radish (or other radish)
- ¼ cup store-bought seaweed salad (see Tip)
- ¼ cup mixed sprouts or microgreens, such as radish or alfalfa
- 2 tablespoons Lime Citronette dressing (page 190)
- 2 avocados, halved, pitted, and peeled
- ¼ cup furikake (see Tip, opposite)

TIP:

Packaged seaweed salad is a common garnish at Japanese restaurants, and it is often available in the ready-to-eat refrigerated section of health food stores. There's no good substitute, so if you can't find it, simply omit it.

1. **MAKE THE DRESSING:** In a blender, combine the vinegar, tahini, sesame oil, sriracha, soy sauce, sugar, salt, ginger, and 2 tablespoons water and blend on high speed until smooth, about 20 seconds. With the motor running, stream in the canola oil until combined, about 20 seconds.

2. **MAKE THE POKE BOWL:** In a medium bowl, toss the brown rice with half of the ginger-sesame dressing. Divide the rice among 4 small bowls and top with the

salmon, edamame, radish, seaweed salad, and sprouts. Drizzle with the Lime Citronette dressing.

3. Set the avocado halves flat-side down on a cutting board. Score each half into cubes without cutting all the way through the avocado (the avocado halves should remain intact to hold the dressing, but precutting the cubes makes for easier eating). Place an avocado half cut-side up on each poke bowl and fill the cavity with the remaining ginger-sesame dressing. Sprinkle with the furikake.

HOW TO: Cook Brown Rice

In a heavy saucepan, bring 1 cup brown rice and 1¾ cups water to a boil over medium-high heat. Reduce the heat to low, cover, and simmer until the rice is tender and the water has been absorbed, 40 to 45 minutes. Fluff gently and let stand, covered, for 10 minutes.

cauliflower velouté

Mark Twain once said, "A cauliflower is nothing but a cabbage with a college education." Twain may have been one of the best writers of his time, but we think he should stay out of the kitchen. Cauliflower is one of our favorite veggies because it's so versatile—plus, it's sneakily a great source of vitamin C. We add raw cauliflower to this velvety smooth velouté to give it some texture. To get it to super-crunchy heights, we dunk raw, thinly sliced cauliflower in an ice bath. If you have any leftover cauliflower, just put it in water and refrigerate it to eat later as a quick snack or salad topper.

SERVES 4

1 large head cauliflower, halved and cored, a handful thinly sliced for serving (1 cup) and the rest cubed

2 cups whole milk, plus more as needed

4 fresh sage leaves

2 sprigs fresh thyme

½ teaspoon salt

1 avocado, pitted, peeled, and quartered, 3 quarters thinly sliced

2 tablespoons Pecan Chermoula (page 187), for topping

1. Bring a large pot of salted water to a boil. Add the cubed cauliflower and cook until tender, about 8 minutes; drain. Return the cooked cauliflower to the pot and add the milk, sage, thyme, and salt; cook over medium heat for about 10 minutes. Remove from the heat, discard the sage and thyme, and add the unsliced quarter of the avocado. Using an immersion blender, blend the cauliflower mixture until smooth. If necessary, add a little more milk or hot water until the soup reaches your desired consistency; it should be creamy but not too thick.

2. To serve, ladle the soup into bowls. Top with the avocado slices and raw cauliflower slices and drizzle with the chermoula.

chilled cucumber soup

Yes, this soup is meant for eating, but it doubles as a hydrating plant-based face mask. Cooling cucumber is known to slow the aging process and is a master at fighting free radical damage. It also helps to keep you hydrated and combats the negative impact of everyday stress. Go ahead and slather it on your face—minus the toppings and dressing, obviously. (Seriously, guys—you totally can. Francesco wore a cucumber soup face mask while he wrote this whole cookbook.)

SERVES 4

4 cups spinach leaves

4 cups diced cucumbers, plus 24 thin slices cucumber

2 avocados, pitted and peeled

2 tablespoons plus 2 teaspoons chopped scallions

1 tablespoon fresh lime juice

2 tablespoons plus 2 teaspoons tahini

2 teaspoons salt

2 tablespoons plus 2 teaspoons hulled pumpkin seeds, toasted

2 tablespoons plus 2 teaspoons Yogurt & Fresh Herbs dressing (page 185)

1. In a blender, combine the spinach, diced cucumbers, 1 of the avocados, the scallions, lime juice, tahini, salt, and ¼ cup water and blend on high speed until smooth, about 30 seconds.

2. Thinly slice the remaining avocado crosswise.

3. To serve, pour the soup into bowls. Top evenly with the avocado slices, cucumber slices, and pumpkin seeds and drizzle with the yogurt dressing.

salmorejo tomato soup

Alberto first tasted this bread soup, served at room temperature, in one of the oldest tapas bars in Seville, Spain. If you want to add an authentic touch, top the soup with salty Serrano ham and hard-boiled egg before serving. But don't forgo the croutons—they give this soup some much-needed texture.

SERVES 4

¼ cup olive oil

2 cloves garlic, crushed

1 teaspoon sweet smoked paprika

4 cups chopped tomatoes

2 avocados, pitted and peeled

1 cup red wine vinegar

½ cup chopped red bell pepper

¼ cup chopped red onion

2 cups torn or diced toasted ciabatta bread pieces

16 Kalamata olives, pitted and halved

Croutons (page 179), for topping

1. In a small saucepan, heat the olive oil over medium heat to 150°F, about 2 minutes. Remove from the heat and add the garlic and paprika; let cool to room temperature. Reserve 4 teaspoons of the oil for topping and transfer the remaining oil and the garlic to a blender.

2. Add the tomatoes, 1 of the avocados, the vinegar, bell pepper, and onion and blend on high speed for 30 seconds. Add the bread and 1 cup water; blend until creamy.

3. Cut the remaining avocado into cubes.

4. To serve, pour the soup into bowls. Top with the avocado cubes, olives, and croutons and drizzle with the reserved garlic oil.

"

This is Alberto's twist on a classic Spanish soup—you certainly won't find avocado in the original!

"

mains

avo burger

We use an entire avocado to make our burger—one of our most popular menu items. Use the better-looking avocado half as the top "bun." To make the bottom "bun" more stable when plated, just cut a thin slice from the rounded side so it sits flat. We recommend tackling this with a fork and knife, but if you're feeling brave, go at it with your hands, and don't forget to take plenty of pictures to showcase your avo-eating skills on Insta.

SERVES 2

2 avocados, pitted and peeled

¼ cup Yogurt & Fresh Herbs dressing (page 185)

1 cup loosely packed arugula, plus more for serving

3 ounces smoked salmon

A few thin slices watermelon radish (or other radish)

2 teaspoons Lime Citronette dressing (page 190)

Olive oil, for drizzling

Black sesame seeds, for sprinkling

1. Place an avocado half, cut-side up, on each of two serving plates and fill the cavity in each with the yogurt dressing. Top with the arugula, salmon, and radish. Drizzle with the citronette dressing and top with the remaining avocado halves. Drizzle with olive oil and sprinkle with sesame seeds.

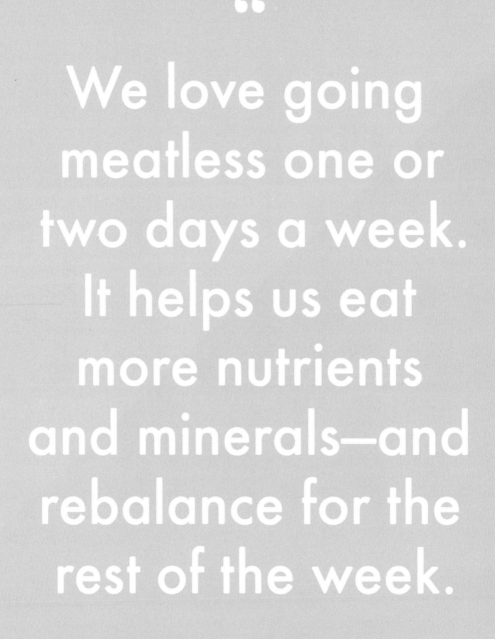

"
We love going
meatless one or
two days a week.
It helps us eat
more nutrients
and minerals—and
rebalance for the
rest of the week.
"

avo-falafel burger

The best part about this recipe—aside from the avocado, of course—is the heart-healthy tahini. Made with sesame seeds, one of the best plant sources of copper, tahini also contains B vitamins, which we have to thank for our glowing skin and Alessandro's gorgeous locks. (Our menu is our main attraction, but Alessandro does have his admirers...) Note that you'll need to soak the dried chickpeas overnight, so plan ahead.

SERVES 3

¼ cup cooked chickpeas (canned are fine), drained and rinsed

½ cup fresh parsley leaves

1 tablespoon olive oil, plus more for coating the burgers

1 tablespoon tahini

2 teaspoons nutritional yeast

1 teaspoon fresh lemon juice

½ teaspoon salt

¼ teaspoon ground cumin

¼ teaspoon sweet smoked paprika

¼ teaspoon baking powder

1 cup dried chickpeas, soaked overnight

1 cup mashed avocado

3 pretzel buns, preferably 4 inches in diameter, split in half and toasted

3 tablespoons Yogurt & Fresh Herbs dressing (page 185)

3 tablespoons Vegan Chipotle & Turmeric Mayo (page 195)

½ cup spicy greens, such as arugula, watercress, and/or mustard greens

1. In a blender, combine the ¼ cup cooked chickpeas, parsley, olive oil, tahini, nutritional yeast, lemon juice, salt, cumin, paprika, and baking powder and blend until combined. Add the drained soaked chickpeas and pulse to form a coarse mixture.

2. Preheat the oven to 375°F. Using a ⅓-cup measure, form the chickpea mixture into 3 patties; flatten each with your hands to about 3½ inches wide. Brush a baking sheet with olive oil, place the burgers on top, and brush them with more olive oil. Bake until golden, about 30 minutes.

3. To serve, spread one-third of the mashed avocado on each pretzel bun bottom. Top each with a falafel patty, 1 teaspoon of the yogurt dressing, 1 teaspoon of the mayo, one-third of the greens, and the pretzel bun tops.

avo tartare

We can understand people being skeeved out at eating beef tartare, which is traditionally made with raw beef and egg yolk, but we do think the French were onto something by celebrating high-quality ingredients with only minimal preparation. We've given avocado the tartare treatment here, and we even serve it using ring molds as in the classic preparation (you can find them in most cookware stores or online); alternatively you can just mound the tartare on the serving plates. Serve the tartare with rice crackers or tortilla chips for the most sophisticated snack ever.

SERVES 2

1 tablespoon plus 1 teaspoon very finely diced celery, plus celery leaves for topping

1 tablespoon plus 1 teaspoon very finely diced jicama

2 teaspoons drained capers in vinegar, finely chopped

1 teaspoon finely chopped fresh parsley leaves

1 teaspoon finely chopped fresh cilantro leaves

1 teaspoon finely chopped scallion

½ teaspoon finely chopped pickled ginger

2 tablespoons olive oil

1 tablespoon plus 1 teaspoon Vegan Soy Mayo (page 196)

2 teaspoons fresh lemon juice

1 teaspoon Dijon mustard

1 avocado, pitted, peeled, and cut into ⅔-inch cubes

1. In a medium bowl, stir together the celery, jicama, capers, parsley, cilantro, scallion, pickled ginger, olive oil, mayo, lemon juice, and mustard. Add the avocado and gently stir to coat.

2. Place a 5-inch metal ring mold on each of two serving plates; divide the avocado mixture between the ring molds, pressing down gently to pack the mixture into the molds.

3. To serve, carefully remove the rings and top the tartare with celery leaves.

mango tuna avo ceviche

Inspired by his time in Mexico, Francesco wanted to serve a mango and avocado ceviche. Alberto decided to do him one better by adding red tuna to make this a satisfying main. Serve the ceviche in the avocado skins for a cool presentation or pile it high over a stack of tortilla chips if you want to maximize your snackage. Roasted corn kernels, such as Corn Nuts or Inka Corn, give the dish a nice crunch.

SERVES 2

FOR THE PICO DE GALLO

3 tablespoons very finely chopped tomatoes

1 tablespoon very finely diced green bell peppers

2 teaspoons chopped scallion

½ teaspoon fresh lime juice

¼ teaspoon chopped fresh cilantro

Pinch of salt

Pinch of black pepper

FOR THE CEVICHE

1 cup cubed sushi-grade raw red tuna

¼ cup ¼-inch cubes mango

2 tablespoons cooked sweet corn kernels

1 avocado, pitted, peeled, and cut into ¾-inch cubes

2 tablespoons roasted corn kernels, for topping

2 tablespoons Lime Citronette dressing (page 190), for drizzling

Tortilla chips, for serving

1. **MAKE THE PICO DE GALLO:** In a medium bowl, toss together the tomatoes, bell peppers, scallion, lime juice, cilantro, salt, and black pepper; set aside for about 10 minutes.

2. **MAKE THE CEVICHE:** Add the tuna, mango, corn, and avocado to the bowl with the pico de gallo and stir together; cover and marinate in the fridge for at least 10 minutes. Transfer to a serving bowl, top with the roasted corn kernels, drizzle with dressing, and serve with tortilla chips.

TIP:

If you're uncertain about which grade of tuna to buy, we suggest visiting your local fish market and having a quick chat with the staff. Although most raw fish is usually lumped together, high-quality fish markets will be careful to store "sushi grade" or "sashimi grade" fish separately from other fish they're selling.

zucchini spaghetti

with avo pesto

Yep, it's true: We're Italian and there's not a single strand of pasta in our cookbook. But when we first came across the idea of "zoodles," we knew we wanted to use them for a twist on an Italian evergreen—pesto. In Italy, traditional pesto isn't made with avocado, but we can't deny that it makes a perfectly creamy sauce.

SERVES 2

FOR THE AVO PESTO

4 cups fresh basil leaves, blanched (see below)

2 tablespoons olive oil

½ teaspoon salt

1 cup grated Parmesan cheese or Cashew Parmesan (page 179)

¼ cup pine nuts

1 avocado, pitted and peeled, half cut into cubes

FOR THE SPAGHETTI

1 teaspoon olive oil, plus more for drizzling

1 clove garlic

32 ounces zoodles (from about 3 medium zucchini)

Salt

Pine nuts, toasted, for topping

Fresh basil leaves, for topping

Grated Parmesan cheese or Cashew Parmesan (page 179), for topping

1. **MAKE THE AVO PESTO:** In a blender or food processor, blend together the blanched basil, olive oil, salt, and ¼ cup water. Add the parmesan, pine nuts, and ½ avocado; process until smooth and creamy.

2. **MAKE THE SPAGHETTI:** In a medium nonstick pan, heat the olive oil and garlic over medium-high heat. Add the zoodles and cook until starting to brown a little, about 3 minutes. Add a pinch of salt and 1 tablespoon water; cook until the zucchini is fork-tender. Divide the zucchini mixture between 2 bowls and top each with the avocado pesto, cubed avocado, pine nuts, basil, and parmesan.

HOW TO: Blanch Basil

Blanching basil prevents oxidation and helps retain its naturally bright green color.

1. Bring a pot of salted water to a boil. Fill a large bowl with ice and water.

2. Submerge the basil in the boiling water and cook for 1 minute.

3. Using a slotted spoon, immediately transfer the basil to the ice bath to cool, then drain on paper towels.

avo, tofu & edamame dumplings

We love dim sum, and there's no shortage of options available in New York City's Chinatown. One of our favorite places to go is Nom Wah Tea Parlor—it's been around for decades and is super old-school in the best way possible. They serve out-of-this-world veggie dumplings, and this is our homage—avo included, of course!—to the Big Apple institution.

MAKES 28 DUMPLINGS

⅔ cup frozen shelled edamame

8 ounces firm tofu, cut into small cubes (1 cup)

3 teaspoons fresh lemon juice

2½ teaspoons toasted sesame oil

1 teaspoon light soy sauce

1 teaspoon finely grated fresh ginger

1 teaspoon finely chopped scallion

½ teaspoon salt

½ avocado, pitted and peeled

28 store-bought wonton wrappers

¼ cup dark soy sauce

1. Bring a pot of salted water to a boil. Add the edamame and boil until cooked but still firm, about 3 minutes. Drain.

2. In a small bowl, mash together the cooked edamame and the tofu with a fork. Stir in 1 teaspoon of the lemon juice, ½ teaspoon of the sesame oil, the light soy sauce, ginger, scallion, and salt until combined. Mash in the avocado.

3. Place 2 teaspoons of the filling down the center of one wonton wrapper; moisten two of the edges lightly with water. Fold the wrapper over and press to seal the edges. Repeat with the remaining wrappers and filling.

4. Line a steamer basket with parchment paper and set it over a pot of simmering water. Steam the dumplings, working in batches if necessary, until the filling is just cooked through, about 5 minutes.

5. Meanwhile, in a small bowl, stir together the dark soy sauce, remaining 2 teaspoons lemon juice, and remaining 2 teaspoons sesame oil; serve as a dipping sauce with the cooked dumplings.

bresaola & avocado carpaccio

with pine nuts & parm

We're always looking for healthy switches for ourselves and our customers. Alberto had the brilliant idea to use lean bresaola, an air-dried, salt-cured meat, instead of a fattier cured meat like prosciutto and to cut down on the amount of Parmesan that's traditionally used in a dish like this. Stupendo.

SERVES 2

12 thin slices (about 3 ounces) bresaola

¼ cup arugula

¼ cup mixed microgreens and sprouts, such as alfalfa, pea, and radish

2 tablespoons Lime Citronette dressing (page 190)

1 firm avocado, pitted, peeled, and cut into very thin slices

2 tablespoons shaved Parmesan cheese

1 tablespoon pine nuts, toasted

1. On a serving platter, arrange the bresaola slices in a single layer.

2. In a bowl, toss together the arugula, microgreens, and sprouts, and 1 tablespoon of the dressing. Top the bresaola with the arugula mixture, avocado, Parmesan, and pine nuts. Drizzle with the remaining 1 tablespoon dressing and serve.

avo crab cakes

The Sunday before Avocaderia's grand opening was Alberto's birthday, so we wandered over to Red Hook, an industrial neighborhood on Brooklyn's waterfront, and ate at Brooklyn Crab, which is famed for its seafood. Their incredible crab cakes inspired this recipe—but, of course, we had to add avocado.

SERVES 4

1 cup claw crabmeat

½ avocado, mashed

1 tablespoon finely chopped scallion

1 tablespoon finely chopped celery

1 teaspoon fresh lime juice

1 tablespoon Vegan Chipotle & Turmeric Mayo (page 195), plus more for serving

Pinch of salt

Pinch of black pepper

1 large egg

1⅓ cups panko bread crumbs

Canola oil, for cooking

Guaca Mayo (page 194), for serving

1. In a medium bowl, combine the crabmeat, avocado, scallion, celery, lime juice, chipotle mayo, salt, pepper, egg, and bread crumbs; cover and refrigerate for at least 1 hour or up to overnight.

2. Divide the crab mixture into 4 large (about ½ cup each) portions.

3. Lightly oil a skillet and heat over medium heat. Add the crab cakes and cook until golden, turning once, about 4 minutes on each side. Serve with Guaca Mayo and additional chipotle mayo.

"

Besides giving these crab cakes their beautiful green color and some healthy fat, avocado keeps everything super moist and tender.

"

roasted vegetable– avo napoleon

A Napoleon, which in Italy we call a *millefoglie*—many leaves— is classically a dessert made of puff pastry sandwiched with sweet cream. Ever the mad genius, Alberto came up with a savory version using roasted vegetables and sliced avocado as the layers. Note that it needs to be refrigerated for at least a couple of hours, or overnight, before serving, so plan ahead; because it's made in advance, it's great for a dinner party or your next romantic date.

SERVES 4

2 cups mixed fresh herb leaves, such as basil, mint, and parsley, coarsely chopped, plus more for topping

2 tablespoons olive oil, plus more for greasing and drizzling

1 tablespoon fresh lemon juice

1 clove garlic, finely chopped

2 teaspoons dried oregano

½ teaspoon salt

¼ teaspoon black pepper

2 red bell peppers

5 medium zucchini, cut lengthwise into ⅛-inch-thick slices

1 medium eggplant, cut crosswise into ¼-inch-thick rounds

2 avocados, sliced

1. In a small bowl, stir together the chopped herbs, olive oil, lemon juice, garlic, oregano, salt, and pepper.

2. Preheat the oven to 400°F and line a baking sheet with foil.

3. Place the bell peppers on the prepared baking sheet and roast, turning occasionally, until the skins are wrinkled and charred, about 30 minutes. Remove the pan from the oven and immediately cover tightly with foil. Let cool, covered, for 30 minutes. Gently peel, stem, and seed the peppers; place in a small bowl with 2 teaspoons of the herb dressing.

4. Working in batches, place the zucchini and eggplant slices on a microwave-safe dish and microwave, covered with a damp paper towel or microwave-safe lid, until tender, about 4 minutes. Generously drizzle the cooked zucchini and eggplant all over with olive oil.

5. Heat a cast-iron skillet over medium-high heat. Working in batches, add the zucchini and eggplant slices and cook until charred, turning once, about 4 minutes total for each batch. Place the zucchini and eggplant in 2 separate small bowls; stir 2 teaspoons herb dressing into each bowl.

6. In a small bowl, gently toss the avocados with the remaining herb dressing.

7. To assemble, line a 9-by-5-inch loaf pan with plastic wrap, leaving about a 2-inch overhang on all sides. Place a layer of avocado slices on the bottom and top with the peppers, zucchini, and eggplant; repeat with the remaining ingredients. Cover with the overhanging plastic wrap and press gently to compact the layers; refrigerate for at least 2 hours or up to overnight.

8. To serve, invert onto a serving platter and remove the plastic wrap; top with fresh herb leaves.

pan-seared salmon-avo onigiri

When Alessandro went to Japan last year to see the famed sakura—cherry blossoms—which bloom very briefly in the spring, of course he also took recipe inspiration from everything he ate. One favorite was *onigiri*, or rice balls. They are ubiquitous in Japan and can be found everywhere from convenience stores to upscale restaurants. Onigiri can be filled with practically anything; salmon and avocado are a delicious combination.

SERVES 2, OR 4 AS AN APPETIZER (MAKES 4 ONIGIRI)

FOR THE RICE

1 cup sushi rice, rinsed in cold water and drained
1 slice fresh ginger
Peel of 1 lemon
2 tablespoons rice vinegar
½ teaspoon salt
½ teaspoon sugar

FOR THE SALMON

1 tablespoon store-bought teriyaki sauce
1 teaspoon shichimi togarashi
Salt
1 skin-on salmon fillet (about 5 ounces)
1 tablespoon canola oil
¼ cup frozen shelled edamame
1 avocado, pitted and peeled
2 teaspoons fresh lemon juice
1 teaspoon toasted sesame oil
2 tablespoons furikake (see Tip, page 87)
4 (4-by-2-inch) pieces nori

1. **MAKE THE RICE:** In a medium saucepan, place the rice and add 1 cup water; cover and bring to a boil over high heat. Reduce the heat to low, cover, and simmer until the water is absorbed and the rice is tender, about 12 minutes. Remove from the heat and gently toss in the ginger and lemon peel; let stand, covered, for about 15 minutes.

2. In a small saucepan set over low heat, or in a small bowl in the microwave, cook the vinegar until warm. Remove from the heat and stir in the salt and sugar until dissolved. Drizzle over the cooked rice and gently toss; transfer to a large bowl or parchment-lined baking sheet and let cool to room temperature. Refrigerate for about 2 hours.

3. **MAKE THE SALMON:** In a small bowl, whisk together the teriyaki sauce, shichimi togarashi, and a pinch of salt. Add the salmon and turn to coat; let marinate for about 15 minutes.

4. In a small skillet, heat the canola oil over medium-high heat. Add the salmon and cook, turning once, about 4 minutes on each side. Remove from the heat, cover, and let sit for about 20 minutes. Remove the skin from the salmon and transfer the fish to a small bowl. Using a fork, break up the fillet into coarse pieces; pour the pan juices on top.

You could also use an onigiri mold to make these, which is the traditional method. Spoon the rice into the mold instead of your cupped palm, layer the ingredients as described, and then press the mold down gently. Remove from the mold, sprinkle with the furikake, and wrap the bottom from front to back with nori.

5. Meanwhile, bring a small pot of salted water to a boil. Blanch the edamame for 4 minutes; drain.

6. In a small bowl, mash together the avocado, lemon juice, and sesame oil with a fork; stir in the edamame and season with salt.

7. Wet your hands to help handle the rice. Spoon 2½ tablespoons rice into your cupped palm and make an indentation in the center. (Alternatively, you can use an onigiri mold; see Tip.) Add about 1 tablespoon of the avocado mash and about 1 tablespoon of salmon mixture; top with 2½ tablespoons rice and press down gently to seal. Transfer to a serving platter and repeat with the remaining ingredients. Sprinkle the onigiri with furikake and press a piece of nori onto the bottom of each.

grilled avocado-shrimp souvlaki

with avo pitas

On a trip to Athens, Alberto had lunch at a tiny, unremarkable-looking place off Omonia Square, where the sole specialty was souvlaki with pita bread. The memory of meat drippings and olive oil soaking into warm pita stayed with Alberto long after his trip was over, and he has re-created the dish many times with various meats and fish. This interpretation with shrimp became his favorite, though. It's perfect for those summer nights when the sun doesn't set until late. We prefer to make our fluffy avo pitas, but to speed things up, go ahead and use your favorite store-bought pitas or flatbread.

SERVES 4 (MAKES 6 SKEWERS AND 4 PITAS)

FOR THE PITA

¼ cup warm water

1 teaspoon sugar

2 teaspoons active dry yeast

2 cups bread flour or all-purpose flour, plus more for dusting

1 teaspoon salt

½ teaspoon baking powder

½ avocado, pitted and peeled

2 tablespoons olive oil

1 tablespoon canola oil, plus more for brushing

FOR THE SOUVLAKI

Zest and juice of ½ lemon

½ teaspoon salt

¼ teaspoon black pepper

1 tablespoon dried oregano

1 tablespoon chopped fresh herbs, such as mint, parsley, and/or thyme

1 clove garlic, crushed

2 teaspoons olive oil

⅓ cup Yogurt & Fresh Herbs dressing (page 185)

18 medium shrimp, peeled and deveined

1 avocado, pitted, peeled, and cut into cubes

Olive oil, for brushing

Dried oregano, for sprinkling

Lemon wedges, for serving

Yogurt & Fresh Herbs dressing (page 185), for dipping

1. **MAKE THE PITA DOUGH:** In a large bowl, stir together the warm water, sugar, and yeast; let sit until frothy, about 10 minutes. In a medium bowl, whisk together the flour, salt, and baking powder.

2. Place the avocado and olive oil in a separate large bowl; using an immersion blender, blend until smooth. Add the avocado mixture and the flour mixture to the bowl with the yeast mixture and stir to combine.

3. On a floured surface, knead the dough for about 4 minutes. Drizzle the canola oil over the dough and roll to completely coat the dough with the oil. Place the dough in a large bowl and cover with plastic wrap; let rise in a warm place until doubled in size, about 1½ hours.

4. While the dough rises, soak 6 bamboo skewers in water for at least 20 minutes.

5. Divide the dough into 4 equal pieces and place on a sheet of parchment paper; cover with a dishtowel and let rise for about 20 minutes.

6. **MEANWHILE, START THE SOUVLAKI:** In a small bowl, stir together the lemon zest, lemon juice, salt, pepper, oregano, fresh herbs, garlic, olive oil, and yogurt dressing. Add the shrimp and let marinate in the fridge for 15 minutes.

7. **COOK THE PITAS:** Shape each piece of dough into an 8-inch round, dusting them lightly with flour if the dough is too sticky to handle. Brush the rounds on both sides with canola oil.

8. Heat a cast-iron skillet over medium-high heat until hot but not smoking. Working with one round of dough at a time, place the dough in the pan and cook for 2 minutes. Cover with a lid and cook until the dough starts to puff up, about 2 minutes more; flip and cook for 2 minutes on the second side. Repeat with the remaining dough.

9. **COOK THE SOUVLAKI:** Remove the shrimp from the marinade; discard the marinade. Drain the skewers and thread 3 shrimp, alternating with 3 avocado cubes, onto each skewer.

10. Heat a cast-iron grill pan over medium heat. Cook the skewers, turning once, until the avocado is charred and the shrimp are opaque, about 2 minutes on each side.

11. To serve, brush the hot pitas with olive oil and sprinkle with oregano. Remove the shrimp and avocado from the skewers and stuff them into the hot pitas. Serve with lemon wedges and more yogurt dressing for dipping.

chia seed–crusted tuna

with avocado and mango-corn salsa

Chia seeds aren't just for pudding anymore, guys. We coat tuna steaks with crunchy chia instead of sesame seeds to get a healthy dose of omega-3s, which are great for your heart. The resulting crust is gorgeous and full of flavor.

SERVES 2

½ cup Mango-Corn Salsa (page 186)

½ avocado, pitted, peeled, and cut into ¼-inch cubes

2 (2-inch-thick) tuna steaks (about 1 pound total)

¼ cup chia seeds

2 teaspoons canola oil

2 teaspoons Maldon sea salt

TIP:

If you're not yet familiar with Maldon sea salt, we suggest you pick up a box immediately. Maldon is flakier and has larger crystals than table salt and lends a distinctive texture and taste to a dish that you just can't achieve with table salt. It's great for adding a finishing touch to a variety of dishes, but we really like using it for seared meats and fishes.

1. In a small bowl, stir together the salsa and avocado.

2. Coat both sides of the tuna steaks with the chia seeds, gently pressing them to adhere to the tuna. In a large skillet, heat the canola oil over medium heat. Add the tuna steaks and sear until golden, about 2 minutes on each side, then hold the steaks with tongs and sear the edges for about 45 seconds each.

3. To serve, cut the tuna into ½-inch-thick slices. Arrange the tuna slices on a platter, sprinkle with the sea salt, and serve with the avocado salsa.

baja fish tacos

The beauty of a truly good fish taco lies in the brightness of its ingredients—the crunch of purple cabbage combined with perfectly flaked fish and our tangy lime dressing really can't be beat, especially on a hot summer day. You can use any white fish for these tacos—ask the guy behind the fish counter for the freshest catch, and you can't go wrong. For even more of a sun-and-surf vibe, do yourself a solid and serve these with our Avo-Colada Smoothie (page 175).

SERVES 4

Juice of 1 lime

1 tablespoon plus 1 teaspoon olive oil

2 teaspoons dried oregano

2 teaspoons sweet smoked paprika

2 teaspoons ground cumin

Pinch of salt

Pinch of black pepper

4 medium white fish fillets, like grouper, halibut, or cod

3 tablespoons Lime Citronette dressing (page 190)

1 tablespoon chopped fresh cilantro

1 teaspoon ground coriander

8 small corn tortillas

1 cup Traditional Guac (page 122)

2 cups mixed julienned vegetables, such as carrot, daikon, and purple cabbage

4 radishes, thinly sliced

1. In a medium bowl, stir together the lime juice, olive oil, oregano, paprika, cumin, salt, and pepper. Add the fish and let marinate for about 15 minutes.

2. Heat a cast-iron skillet over high heat. Place the fish and the marinade in the pan and cook until the liquid is reduced and the fish is golden, turning once, about 4 minutes on each side. Break the fish into big chunks.

3. Meanwhile, in a small bowl, stir together the Lime Citronette, cilantro, and coriander.

4. Heat a nonstick pan over medium heat. Working in batches, cook the tortillas until warmed, turning once, about 2 minutes on each side.

5. To assemble, spread 2 tablespoons guac in the center of each tortilla and top with 2 to 3 fish chunks, some of the julienned vegetables, and some radish slices. Drizzle with the lime-cilantro dressing.

apps + sides

traditional guac

After tasting guacamole for the first time in Mexico, Alberto ended up eating it every day on the beach until he had to return home to Italy. Not much has changed since then—he's always ready for a guac-fest when the time calls for it, which is pretty much always, in our opinion.

MAKES ABOUT 4 CUPS

4 avocados, pitted and peeled

½ jalapeño, seeded and chopped

2 tomatoes, chopped

3 scallions, white and green parts, chopped

2½ tablespoons fresh lime juice

1 teaspoon salt, plus more to taste

Tortilla chips or pita chips, for serving

1. In a large bowl, mash the avocados coarsely with a fork.

2. In a food processor, pulse together the jalapeño, tomatoes, scallions, lime juice, and salt until salsa-like in texture. Add the tomato mixture to the bowl with the avocados and stir to combine. Serve with tortilla chips or pita chips.

3. If not serving immediately, press plastic wrap directly against the surface of the guac to prevent browning and refrigerate until ready to serve, up to overnight.

"

When Alberto was fourteen years old, he had his first taste of guacamole in Mexico. Who could have known that first taste would eventually lead him to Avocaderia?

"

signature guac

When we opened our first Avocaderia location, we were living in Sunset Park, Brooklyn, a neighborhood populated with tiny Mexican food shops. There, Alberto discovered ingredients that were new and exciting—at least to him. One of his favorite finds was jicama, a Mexican vegetable similar to a large radish. Alberto loves jicama's crunchy texture, and combined it with cucumber and celery to make our signature guac so unique and so, so good. When we first opened shop, our customers were confused by the unexpected ingredients, but they ended up loving this refreshing version. We have many regulars who now refuse to eat guac any other way!

MAKES ABOUT 4 CUPS

4 avocados, pitted and peeled

¼ cup plus 2 tablespoons Green Pico (page 186)

3 tablespoons Lime Citronette dressing (page 190)

Maldon sea salt, for sprinkling

Tortilla chips or pita chips, for serving

1. In a large bowl, mash the avocados coarsely with a fork. Add the pico, dressing, and a sprinkle of sea salt; stir to combine. Serve with tortilla chips or pita chips.

2. If not serving immediately, press plastic wrap directly against the surface of the guac to prevent browning and refrigerate until ready to serve, up to overnight.

pickled avo & cucumber wedges
in spiced brine

Italians love preserving their harvest—and avocados are no exception. For this recipe, we suggest using an unripe avocado so it will hold up in the brine (see Avocado 101 on page 19 for how to tell when an avo is ripe). Go ahead and add different flavoring agents, like black peppercorns, chiles, citrus zest, or even cinnamon, to the brine. These guys will keep in the fridge for up to three days, but we've never been able to keep them around that long!

SERVES 2

1 tablespoon sugar

2 teaspoons salt

½ cup apple cider vinegar

1 star anise pod

½ teaspoon Sichuan peppercorns

2 slices fresh ginger

2 small cucumbers (about 4 inches long), quartered lengthwise

½ unripe avocado, pitted, peeled, and sliced into 5 wedges

1. In a small saucepan, heat 1 cup water, the sugar, and the salt over medium heat, stirring to dissolve the sugar and salt. Stir in the vinegar, star anise, peppercorns, and ginger; remove from the heat.

2. Place the cucumbers and avocado in a glass jar. Pour over the warm brine and cover with plastic wrap or the jar's lid. Let cool to room temperature, seal the jar, then refrigerate for at least 3 hours or up to overnight. The pickles will keep in the refrigerator for up to 3 days.

stuffed avo
with puffed quinoa & spiced crust

We serve this stuffed avocado as is or over a spicy green salad. The star ingredient? Shichimi togarashi—a classic Japanese table condiment made of red chile, sesame seeds, ginger, seaweed, and roasted orange peel. To balance out the shichimi, we fill the avocado with our cooling yogurt spread.

SERVES 2

½ cup puffed quinoa

1 tablespoon Spiced Seeds (page 178)

1 tablespoon Pistachio Dukkah (page 178)

1 teaspoon shichimi togarashi

1 avocado, halved and pitted

Olive oil, for brushing

¼ cup Yogurt & Fresh Herbs dressing (page 185)

1. Spread the puffed quinoa in a shallow layer on a small plate. Combine the spiced seeds, dukkah, and shichimi togarashi in a small bowl.

2. Brush the flat surface of each avocado half with olive oil. Flip it onto the quinoa and press to coat with a layer of quinoa. Flip the avocado back over and set it on a plate.

3. Sprinkle the avocados with the spiced seed mixture and then fill each half with the yogurt dressing.

guac tots

with pico de gallo

Freezing the avocado filling first ensures perfectly shaped tots and makes frying a cinch. You can prepare the tots ahead of time and freeze them for later; they'll keep for up to three months. They're great to pull out for casual get-togethers—in fact, at our last Super Bowl party, we were dubbed the Snack Winners for these guys. Be careful, though: Kids and adults both love them, and these tots go fast! We suggest tripling or even quadrupling this recipe if you're serving a large crowd. Don't say we didn't warn you . . .

SERVES 2 (MAKES 7 TOTS)

FOR THE PICO DE GALLO

- ¾ cup diced tomatoes
- ⅓ cup diced green bell peppers
- ¼ cup finely chopped scallions (white and green parts)
- ¼ teaspoon finely chopped fresh cilantro
- 2 teaspoons fresh lime juice
- ½ teaspoon salt
- Pinch of black pepper

FOR THE TOTS

- 1 avocado, pitted, peeled, and mashed
- 1 teaspoon fresh lime juice
- 2 teaspoons olive oil
- ¼ teaspoon salt, plus a pinch
- Vegetable oil, for frying
- 2 tablespoons nutritional yeast
- ¼ cup cornstarch
- 2 cups old-fashioned rolled oats

1. **MAKE THE PICO DE GALLO:** In a small bowl, stir together the tomatoes, bell peppers, scallions, cilantro, lime juice, ½ teaspoon salt, and black pepper.

2. **MAKE THE TOTS:** In a small bowl, mix together the avocado, lime juice, olive oil, and ¼ teaspoon salt.

3. Line a baking sheet with parchment paper. Portion out seven 2-tablespoon scoops of the avocado mixture onto the prepared baking sheet; freeze for at least 30 minutes and up to 2 hours. To freeze the uncooked tots for up to 3 months, transfer the frozen tots to an airtight container or resealable bag.

4. Fill a large pot with vegetable oil to a depth of about 3 inches. Heat the oil to 350°F. In a medium bowl, whisk together the nutritional yeast, cornstarch, 3 tablespoons water, and a pinch of salt until smooth. Put the oats in a bowl.

5. Using a toothpick, first dip the frozen tots in the cornstarch batter, then in the oats. Set aside on a plate and bread the remaining tots. Fry the tots until golden brown, about 3 minutes. Drain on a paper towel–lined plate before serving.

6. Serve hot with the pico de gallo alongside.

guac-loaded sweet potatoes

Baked potatoes loaded down with bacon and sour cream aren't really our jam (sorry, Idaho!). We much prefer this healthier take using sweet potatoes, which are gold mines for potassium and beta-carotene. Not to brag, but we think you'll never go back once you try our version . . .

SERVES 2

2 medium sweet potatoes

2 teaspoons olive oil

2 teaspoons Maldon sea salt

¼ teaspoon black pepper

⅔ cup Signature Guac (page 125)

¼ cup pico de gallo (see page 130)

2 tablespoons Vegan Chipotle & Turmeric Mayo (page 195), for drizzling

2 tablespoons crunchy fried corn (such as Corn Nuts or Inka Corn), crushed, for topping

Cilantro leaves, for topping

1. Preheat the oven to 400°F.

2. Pierce each sweet potato several times with a fork and place on a baking sheet; bake until tender, about 50 minutes. Let cool for about 10 minutes.

3. Make a slit in the top of each sweet potato and season with the olive oil, salt, and pepper. Top with the guac and pico de gallo.

4. To serve, drizzle with the mayo and top with the corn and cilantro.

pinzimonio
with blue cheese-avo dip

We might be a tad biased, but we think the Italian language is beautiful (we *definitely, absolutely* have never used it to impress ladies . . .). So it's not surprising that Italians came up with such an elegant word for what is basically a veggie platter. Pinzimonio is an Italian-style crudités featuring crunchy vegetables like endive, fennel, and carrots. Don't stress if you don't have these on hand—use your imagination and dunk whatever you have in the fridge into this sharp, tangy dip. Pita chips work amazingly well here, too.

SERVES 4

1½ ounces (3 tablespoons) crumbled blue cheese

½ avocado, pitted and peeled

¼ cup pecans

3 tablespoons olive oil

1 teaspoon red wine vinegar

1 teaspoon Dijon mustard

¼ teaspoon salt

Pinch of black pepper

2 Belgian endives, bottoms trimmed and leaves separated

4 stalks celery, cut into sticks

3 carrots, preferably various colors, cut into sticks

1 fennel bulb, cut into 12 segments

8 radishes, halved or quartered

1. In a blender, combine the blue cheese, avocado, pecans, olive oil, vinegar, mustard, salt, and pepper and process on high speed until smooth, about 25 seconds. Transfer to a serving bowl and serve with the vegetables.

Avo Deviled Eggs
(page 141)

Pickled Avo
& Cucumber
Wedges in
Spiced Brine
(page 126)

Stuffed Avo with
Puffed Quinoa &
Spiced Crust
(page 129)

Sweet Potato–
Avo Salad
(page 137)

Signature Guac
(page 125)

sweet potato–avo salad

One humid summer night in Brooklyn, we discovered the joys of barbecue at a no-frills rib joint. Now, Italians like to say that Italy has the best food in the world, but we will admit that American barbecue gives Italy a run for its money. Along with the delights of ribs and pulled pork, we came across barbecue's classic side dishes—coleslaw, baked beans, and potato salad. The potato salad is really what made an impression on Alberto. He went back into the kitchen and produced his own spin on the picnic table favorite—big chunks of avocado, regular and sweet potatoes, and capers for a wonderful acidity. Pair this with an avo-falafel burger (page 99) and you won't even be missing those ribs.

SERVES 2

1 cup fresh parsley leaves

2 tablespoons olive oil

½ teaspoon salt

¼ cup mayonnaise or Vegan Soy Mayo (page 196)

1 teaspoon Dijon mustard

2 teaspoons drained capers in vinegar

2 teaspoons chopped scallions (white and green parts)

2 tablespoons finely chopped celery

1 medium white sweet potato, cooked and cut into ¾-inch cubes (1 cup)

1 medium Idaho or russet potato, cooked and cut into ¾-inch cubes (⅔ cup)

1 avocado, pitted, peeled, and cut into ¾-inch cubes

1. Blanch the parsley for 2 minutes, following the directions on page 104; drain. In a blender, combine the blanched parsley, olive oil, salt, and ¼ cup water and blend until smooth.

2. In a small bowl, stir together 2 tablespoons of the parsley mixture, the mayo, mustard, capers, scallions, and celery. Toss with the cooked potatoes and avocado in a medium bowl.

panko-crusted avo wedges

with tangerine sweet & sour dipping sauce

We mix and match Chinese and Japanese ingredients in this unique avocado side dish. For our housemade sweet-and-sour sauce, we swap in citrusy tangerine juice for the more classic pineapple juice, and for the avo wedges we use light and flaky Japanese panko in place of bread crumbs.

SERVES 2 (MAKES 6 WEDGES)

FOR THE DIPPING SAUCE

- 1 teaspoon cornstarch
- ¼ cup fresh tangerine juice
- 2 tablespoons unseasoned rice vinegar or apple cider vinegar
- 1 tablespoon sugar
- ½ teaspoon Aleppo pepper flakes
- ½ teaspoon sriracha
- ½ teaspoon tangerine zest

FOR THE WEDGES

- Olive oil spray, for coating
- 1 cup panko bread crumbs
- 2 tablespoons nutritional yeast
- ¼ cup cornstarch
- ½ avocado, pitted, peeled, cut into 6 wedges, and frozen for 30 minutes
- Aleppo pepper flakes, for sprinkling

1. **MAKE THE DIPPING SAUCE:** In a small saucepan, whisk together the cornstarch and ¼ cup water until combined. Whisk in the tangerine juice, vinegar, sugar, Aleppo pepper, and sriracha; bring to a boil, stirring continuously, and cook until thickened, about 2 minutes. Stir in the tangerine zest and remove from the heat.

2. **MAKE THE WEDGES:** Preheat the oven to 375°F. Line a baking sheet with parchment paper and coat the parchment with olive oil spray.

3. Put the panko in a shallow bowl. In a medium bowl, whisk together the nutritional yeast, cornstarch, and 3 tablespoons water until smooth to make a batter. Submerge each frozen avocado wedge in the batter, then coat completely with the panko. Place the wedges on the prepared baking sheet and spray with olive oil spray. Bake until crisp, about 20 minutes.

4. Sprinkle with Aleppo pepper and serve with the dipping sauce.

avo deviled eggs

If this doesn't impress your friends at brunch, nothing will— and you probably shouldn't be friends with them anymore. (Just kidding! We guarantee they'll be impressed.) Alberto figured out that with all the beets we boil for salads and toasts, we had leftover naturally colored purple cooking water. He decided to use it as a marinade to give these eggs incredible color. We've streamlined that process here so you don't have to cook a separate beet dish in order to make these stunners. We like to serve these alongside our avo pancakes (page 28) so nobody ever leaves the table hungry.

SERVES 3 (MAKES 6 DEVILED EGGS)

FOR THE BEET MARINADE

1 medium beet, cooked (see page 74) and cut into small cubes

1 tablespoon apple cider vinegar

1 teaspoon salt

FOR THE DEVILED EGGS

3 eggs, hard-boiled and peeled (see page 142)

½ avocado, pitted and peeled

2 teaspoons olive oil

2 teaspoons fresh lime juice

½ teaspoon Dijon mustard

¼ teaspoon black pepper

1 teaspoon beetroot powder (optional)

½ teaspoon sweet smoked paprika

1. **MAKE THE BEET MARINADE:** In a blender, combine the beet, vinegar, salt, and ½ cup water and blend until well combined. Pour the marinade into a medium bowl.

2. **MAKE THE DEVILED EGGS:** Place the eggs in the beet marinade; cover and refrigerate for at least 3 hours or up to overnight. Rinse the eggs under cold running water. Halve the eggs lengthwise and remove the yolks.

3. In a blender or food processor (a mini food processor is ideal, or you can use a fork), blend together the yolks, avocado, olive oil, lime juice, mustard, pepper, and 1 tablespoon water until smooth. Transfer the egg yolk mixture to a piping bag fitted with a medium-size round tip. Place the egg white halves cut-side up on a platter and pipe enough of the egg yolk mixture into the centers to fill. (Alternatively, use a spoon to fill the centers instead of piping.)

(recipe continues)

4. In a small bowl, mix together the beetroot powder and paprika; using a fine-mesh strainer, dust the mixture over the eggs.

HOW TO: Hard-Boil Eggs

1. Place the eggs in a saucepan and add enough water to cover by 2 inches; bring to a boil.

2. When the water comes to a boil, cover the saucepan with a tight-fitting lid and cook for 1 minute.

3. Remove from the heat and set aside, covered, for 13 minutes. Transfer the eggs to a bowl of cold or ice water and let cool.

4. Gently crack and peel the eggs.

grilled corn

with avocado, smoked chipotle & lemon butter

This is the quintessential summer side dish; it's so good that we could eat this all by itself. Prepare the butter ahead of time and keep it in the fridge. Just remember to let the butter sit at room temperature for at least 15 to 20 minutes before serving. For the corn, peel back the husks, remove the silks, and then fold the husks back into place—they'll protect the corn from charring too quickly on the grill.

SERVES 4

1 lemon, halved

8 tablespoons (1 stick) butter, cut into small cubes, at room temperature

½ avocado, pitted and peeled

1 teaspoon sweet smoked paprika, plus more for topping

1 teaspoon salt

½ teaspoon smoked chipotle powder

4 ears fresh corn, husks on but silks removed (see note above), soaked in cold water for 30 minutes

Olive oil

Fresh cilantro leaves (optional)

1. Heat a grill to medium. Place the lemon halves on the grill, flesh-side down, and char, about 3 minutes; let cool. Keep the grill hot.

2. In a food processor, combine the butter, avocado, paprika, salt, chipotle powder, and the juice of one charred lemon half; pulse until combined.

3. Remove the corn from the cold water and place it on the grill. Close the lid and grill until tender, about 8 minutes, turning once about halfway through. Remove the corn from the grill, pull back the husks, and continue grilling, turning, until charred all over, about 6 minutes more.

4. Place the corn on a serving platter and generously brush with half the avocado butter. Drizzle the corn with olive oil and sprinkle with cilantro, if desired, and smoked paprika. Serve with the remaining charred lemon half and remaining avocado butter.

TIP:

You'll notice that we don't use much cilantro in our recipes—that's because Alessandro absolutely despises it. It's actually one of the most polarizing herbs out there, because many people are genetically predisposed to dislike cilantro. Many report that it tastes like soap. Next time you and your friends fight about whether to include cilantro in the guac, remember that your genes may have determined whether or not you'll enjoy the herb long before you've ever actually tried it.

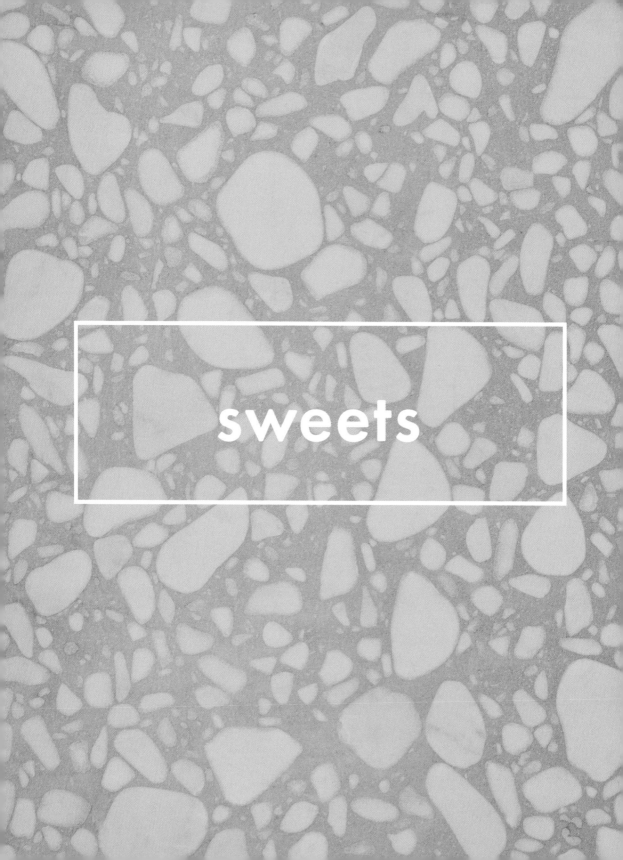

sweets

avo-chocolate mousse

This is the first dessert we ever served at Avocaderia. We initially used almond milk, but after discovering that one of our staff members was allergic to almonds, we swapped in coconut milk and loved the result, which is still vegan and dairy-free. Store the mousse in a resealable container in the refrigerator for up to 2 days.

SERVES 4

1¼ cups unsweetened almond milk or canned coconut milk

1 pound dairy-free dark chocolate, preferably 60% cacao, coarsely chopped

4 small ripe avocados, pitted, peeled, and chopped

¼ cup agave syrup

1 tablespoon finely grated orange zest

2 tablespoons puffed quinoa, for sprinkling

2 teaspoons Maldon sea salt, for sprinkling

2 teaspoons Aleppo pepper flakes, for sprinkling

1 tablespoon extra-virgin olive oil, for drizzling

1. In a small saucepan, heat the almond milk over medium-high heat until it registers 175°F on an instant-read thermometer. Remove from the heat and stir in the chopped chocolate until melted; let cool to room temperature.

2. In a blender, combine the avocados, agave, orange zest, and cooled chocolate mixture and blend on high speed until smooth.

3. To serve, divide the mixture among four bowls. Sprinkle evenly with the puffed quinoa, sea salt, and Aleppo pepper and drizzle with the olive oil.

avo "seed" chocolate truffles

These sweets re-create an avocado pit with chocolate. To get super-luscious truffles, we replaced the traditional heavy cream with avocado. Want to go the extra mile and make these vegan? Just use dairy-free chocolate chips. Choose between the coconut-chocolate, matcha-almond, or coffee-peanut truffles—or do what we do and make all three! (If you choose to make only one flavor, triple the flavoring ingredients.)

MAKES 12 TRUFFLES (4 OF EACH FLAVOR)

FOR THE AVOCADO BASE

½ avocado, pitted and peeled

2 tablespoons agave syrup

FOR THE COCONUT-CHOCOLATE TRUFFLES

3 tablespoons canned unsweetened full-fat coconut milk

1 tablespoon cacao butter

⅓ cup dark chocolate chips, preferably 60% cacao

Unsweetened cacao powder, for coating

Raw cacao nibs, for coating

FOR THE MATCHA-ALMOND TRUFFLES

3 tablespoons unsweetened almond milk

1 tablespoon cacao butter

⅓ cup white chocolate chips

Matcha green tea powder, for coating

FOR THE COFFEE-PEANUT TRUFFLES

¼ cup brewed espresso

1 tablespoon cacao butter

2 teaspoons packed dark brown sugar

3 tablespoons smooth peanut butter

⅓ cup dark chocolate chips, preferably 60% cacao

Crushed coffee beans, for coating

Crushed caramelized peanuts, for coating

1. **MAKE THE AVOCADO BASE:** In a mini food processor, or using an immersion blender, blend the avocado and agave on high speed until combined; refrigerate until ready to use.

2. **MAKE THE COCONUT-CHOCOLATE TRUFFLES:** In a small saucepan, whisk together the coconut milk, cacao butter, and chocolate chips over medium heat until melted and well combined. Remove from the heat and whisk in 2 tablespoons of the avocado base

(recipe continues)

Matcha-Almond
Truffles

Coconut-
Chocolate
Truffles

Coffee-Peanut
Truffles

until combined; refrigerate for at least 3 hours. Place the cacao powder and cacao nibs in two separate small bowls. Using an ice cream scoop, portion out scoops (about 2 tablespoons each) of the chocolate mixture into the cacao powder and turn to coat; transfer to the bowl with the cacao nibs and turn to coat. Refrigerate until ready to serve.

3. **MAKE THE MATCHA-ALMOND TRUFFLES:** In a small saucepan, whisk together the almond milk, cacao butter, and white chocolate chips over medium heat until melted and well combined. Remove from the heat and whisk in 2 tablespoons of the avocado base until combined; refrigerate for at least 3 hours. Place the matcha in a small bowl. Using an ice cream scoop, portion out scoops (about 2 tablespoons each) of the white chocolate mixture into the matcha powder and turn to coat. Refrigerate until ready to serve.

4. **MAKE THE COFFEE-PEANUT TRUFFLES:** In a small saucepan, whisk together the espresso, cacao butter, and brown sugar over medium heat until well combined. Remove from the heat and whisk in 2 tablespoons of the avocado base, the peanut butter, and chocolate chips until combined; refrigerate for at least 3 hours. Place the coffee beans and caramelized peanuts in two separate small bowls. Using an ice cream scoop, portion out scoops (about 2 tablespoons each) of the espresso mixture into the crushed coffee beans and turn to coat; transfer to the bowl with the peanuts and turn to coat. Refrigerate until ready to serve.

"

Cacao butter,
the cold-pressed
oil of cacao beans,
gives the truffles
lots of richness—
and a boost of
healthy fat and
antioxidants.

"

avo-lime cheesecake

This dessert isn't just easy to make—it's a showstopper and promises happy eaters, whether you're at a potluck or a fancy dinner party. The combination of thick yogurt, cream cheese, and avocado makes this cheesecake extra creamy, while the white chocolate in the crust keeps the base crunchy for days. Want to have some fun with this dish? Serve it at your next party and have your guests try to guess the secret ingredient.

SERVES 4

1 tablespoon plus 1 teaspoon white chocolate chips

1 tablespoon plus 1 teaspoon coconut oil

⅔ cup finely crushed oat cookies, such as McVitie's Digestive Biscuits

½ cup whole milk

2 teaspoons unflavored powdered gelatin

⅔ cup cream cheese, at room temperature

1 avocado, pitted and peeled

¼ cup plain Greek yogurt

½ cup superfine sugar

1 tablespoon plus 1 teaspoon fresh lime juice

Zest of 2 limes, plus more for topping

1. Line a baking sheet with parchment paper and place four 4-inch baking molds on top. (Alternatively, you can use four small springform pans or tart pans; line them with parchment paper.)

2. In a small saucepan, melt the white chocolate chips and the coconut oil over medium heat. Stir in the cookie crumbs. Divide the cookie mixture between the prepared molds, pressing it firmly into a layer over the bottom; freeze until firm, at least 15 minutes.

3. Meanwhile, in a small saucepan, stir together the milk and gelatin over medium heat until the gelatin has dissolved.

4. In a blender or food processor, combine the cream cheese, avocado, yogurt, sugar, lime juice, and the gelatin mixture and blend until smooth. Stir in the lime zest. Fill the baking molds with the cream cheese mixture. Refrigerate overnight or for at least 2 hours to set.

5. To serve, unmold the cheesecakes onto individual plates and sprinkle with lime zest.

spread the love shortbread cookie thins

Okay, fine—technically, there's no avocado in these cookies, but you'll forgive us once you taste them. We use matcha powder—ground green tea—because it's a nutritional powerhouse, so you can indulge without feeling guilty. To make matcha, green tea leaves are stone-ground into a superfine powder, which delivers more antioxidants and vitamins, including vitamin C and magnesium, than a cup of regularly brewed green tea. Need a personalized cookie stamp? We found ours on Amazon.com.

MAKES 10 COOKIES

5 tablespoons cold unsalted butter, 3 tablespoons cubed

2 teaspoons matcha green tea powder

⅔ cup all-purpose flour

½ cup confectioners' sugar

Pinch of salt

2 large egg yolks

1. In a small saucepan, melt the 2 tablespoons un-cubed butter. Remove from the heat and stir in the matcha to dissolve; let cool.

2. In a small bowl, sift together the flour and confectioners' sugar. Use a pastry blender to cut in the remaining 3 tablespoons butter until the mixture forms coarse crumbs. Add the salt, egg yolks, and cooled matcha mixture and stir to combine. Wrap the dough in plastic wrap, flatten slightly, and refrigerate for at least 2 hours or up to overnight.

3. Preheat the oven to 350°F.

4. Set the dough on a piece of lightly floured parchment paper and roll it out to about ⅙ inch thick. Transfer the dough, on the parchment paper, to a baking sheet; bake for 12 minutes. Remove from the oven and, while still hot, cut into 4 by 1½-inch pieces; using a cookie stamp, stamp each cookie. Let cool completely on a wire rack. Store the cookies in an airtight container for up to 2 weeks.

avo paletas

These paletas are super high in healthy fats and are the perfect healthy alternative to sugary ice pops. They're also super filling, so try snacking on one of these instead of reaching for the junk food. For extra-creamy pops, we add cashew butter to the mix. Want to take them to the next level? After they're fully frozen, dip the paletas in melted chocolate, then coat with crushed nuts or espresso beans.

MAKES 4 POPS

1 avocado, pitted and
  peeled
½ cup cashew milk
2 tablespoons plus
  2 teaspoons agave syrup
2 tablespoons cashew
  butter
1 tablespoon plus
  1 teaspoon fresh lime
  juice

1. In a blender, combine the avocado, cashew milk, agave, cashew butter, and lime juice and blend on high speed until smooth. Transfer to ice pop molds and insert sticks; freeze until firm, at least 4 hours. Store in the freezer for up to 1 month.

no-churn avo ice cream

This ice cream is packed with avocado and is really simple to make—no ice cream machine required. The combination of condensed milk, coconut milk "cream," heavy cream, and, of course, avocado, prevents the ice cream from forming ice crystals and makes it ridiculously creamy. For even more flavor, add some fresh mint, Thai basil, or lemongrass to the mix.

MAKES 1 QUART

1 avocado, pitted and peeled

¾ cup sweetened condensed milk

1 teaspoon grated lime zest

2 tablespoons fresh lime juice

½ teaspoon grated fresh ginger

¼ vanilla bean, split and seeds scraped, or ½ teaspoon pure vanilla extract

½ cup cold coconut milk "cream" (see at right)

⅔ cup cold heavy cream

Toasted coconut flakes, for sprinkling

1. In a blender, combine the avocado, condensed milk, lime zest, lime juice, ginger, and vanilla seeds and blend on high speed until smooth.

2. In a large bowl, whisk together the coconut milk "cream" and heavy cream until whipped and fluffy. (You can do this by hand or using an electric mixer.) Fold in the avocado mixture. Transfer to a freezer-safe container; freeze for at least 4 hours or overnight. Store in an airtight freezer-safe container for up to 1 month.

3. Serve sprinkled with toasted coconut flakes.

> ## HOW TO: Separate Coconut Milk into "Cream" and "Water"
>
> 1. The day before you want to use the "cream," refrigerate 1 (13.5-ounce) can full-fat coconut milk; let chill overnight.
>
> 2. The next day, open the can; the thick coconut "cream" will have separated from the watery coconut liquid.
>
> 3. Spoon off the cream from the top and use as needed.

avo-chocolate sponge cake
with mint-avo whipped cream

As a kid, Alberto loved stockpiling After Eight candies from restaurants (think Andes mints in fishbowls but for the European market). To re-create that classic chocolate-mint combination, he came up with this satisfying, not-overly-sweet confection, which tastes amazing at any time of day.

SERVES 8

FOR THE SPONGE CAKE

¼ cup superfine sugar

1 cup dark chocolate chips

1 avocado, pitted, peeled, and mashed (about ⅔ cup)

2 tablespoons extra-virgin olive oil

2 tablespoons avocado oil

4 large eggs, at room temperature, beaten

½ cup high-quality unsweetened cocoa powder

2 tablespoons almond flour

2 tablespoons cacao nibs

1 teaspoon baking soda

1 teaspoon baking powder

Pinch of salt

¼ teaspoon pure vanilla extract

FOR THE WHIPPED CREAM

⅓ cup superfine sugar

½ cup fresh mint leaves (about 20)

1 cup cold heavy cream

½ avocado, pitted and peeled

1. **MAKE THE SPONGE CAKE:** Preheat the oven to 375°F. Line an 8-inch square baking pan with parchment paper.

2. In a small saucepan, combine the sugar and 3 tablespoons water and heat over low heat until the sugar has dissolved; let cool to room temperature.

3. Melt ½ cup of the chocolate chips in the microwave or in a heatproof bowl set over a saucepan of simmering water.

4. Place the avocado, sugar syrup, olive oil, and avocado oil in a large bowl; using an immersion blender, blend until pureed. Whisk in the eggs.

5. In a separate bowl, combine the cacao powder, almond flour, cacao nibs, baking soda, baking powder, and salt; fold the cacao mixture into the wet ingredients to combine. Fold in the melted chocolate and the remaining ½ cup chocolate chips. Transfer to the prepared pan and bake until a toothpick inserted into the center comes out clean, about 35 minutes. Let cool on a wire rack for at least 30 minutes. The unfrosted cake will keep in an airtight container for up to 3 days.

6. **MEANWHILE, MAKE THE WHIPPED CREAM:** In a small saucepan, combine the sugar and ⅓ cup water and heat over low heat until the sugar has dissolved. Remove from the heat and stir in the mint leaves. Let cool to room temperature, then discard the mint.

7. In a blender, combine the mint syrup, cream, and avocado and blend on high speed until creamy and whipped, about 25 seconds.

8. Serve the cake topped with the whipped cream.

"

Like crème brûlée, these caramelized avocado wedges have that swoon-worthy crackly sugar on top.

"

caramelized avocado wedges

with spiced seeds & dulce de leche

We didn't think caramelizing an avocado would ever work, but Alberto is a mad scientist in the kitchen and he actually pulled it off. We like to finish these by drizzling them with thick, rich dulce de leche—which is found in Mexico and other Spanish-speaking countries and is similar to caramel—to balance out the fruity avocado.

SERVES 2

1 firm avocado, pitted, peeled, and quartered

2 tablespoons superfine sugar

4 scoops No-Churn Avo Ice Cream (page 158) or vanilla ice cream

4 tablespoons Spiced Seeds (page 178)

2 tablespoons dulce de leche

1. Freeze the avocado wedges for about 15 minutes.

2. Meanwhile, in a small nonstick pan, combine the sugar and 2 teaspoons water and heat over medium heat until the sugar has dissolved; continue to cook, without stirring, until the caramel reaches a medium brown color.

3. Place the avocado wedges, flesh-side down, in the caramel and cook until caramelized, about 1 minute on each side; remove from the heat. Serve with the ice cream, sprinkled with the spiced seeds and drizzled with dulce de leche.

drinks + smoothies

earl grey– hibiscus iced tea

At the shop, we make our botanical iced teas fresh daily. For this one, we combine tart, ruby-red hibiscus flowers—the star ingredient in one of Mexico's most popular agua frescas, agua de Jamaica—with traditional English Earl Grey tea, famous for its bold bergamot orange flavor. The result? A refreshingly fragrant and floral citrusy summer cooler.

MAKES ABOUT 8 CUPS

½ cup loose Earl Grey tea
¾ cup dried hibiscus flowers
Ice, for serving

1. In a pot, heat 8 cups water over high heat until hot but not boiling, or until the temperature reaches 195°F on an instant-read thermometer. Remove from the heat, stir in the tea and flowers, and let steep at room temperature for at least 4 hours or up to overnight. Strain into a large pitcher and refrigerate until chilled. Serve over ice.

---

1 Earl Grey-Hibiscus Iced Tea   **2** Ginger-Mint Lemonade (page 168)
3 Matcha-Kale Green Smoothie (page 173)   **4** Vanilla-Almond Smoothie (page 172)   **5** Avo-Colada Smoothie (page 175)   **6** Avo-Mango Smoothie (page 169)

ginger-mint lemonade

Every day in-house we squeeze a box of fresh lemons and reserve the peels, which are rich in essential oils, to infuse our lemonade. The first week we opened, we had so many lemonade orders that our electric citrus squeezer died. For the next few days, we had to squeeze all the lemons by hand—ow! Mint has cooling, energy-boosting properties, while tangy, spicy ginger has warming, anti-inflammatory qualities, giving this lemonade—and your body on a hot summer day—essential balance.

MAKES ABOUT 8 CUPS

¾ cup sugar

1 cup fresh mint leaves

½ cup coarsely chopped fresh ginger

Zest of 1 lemon, removed in strips with a vegetable peeler

2 cups fresh lemon juice (from about 16 lemons)

Ice cubes, for serving

1. In a small saucepan, stir together the sugar and 1 cup water; bring to a boil, then simmer until the sugar has dissolved. Remove from the heat and stir in ½ cup of the mint; let cool to room temperature. Remove and discard the mint leaves.

2. Place 2 cups water and the ginger in a blender and blend on high speed for about 30 seconds, until mostly smooth; strain the ginger water through a fine-mesh sieve into a large pitcher.

3. Stir in the lemon zest strips, lemon juice, and mint syrup; refrigerate until chilled. Before serving, stir in the remaining ½ cup mint. Serve over ice.

avo-mango smoothie

We make it easy to embrace the all-avo lifestyle by serving our bestselling smoothie year-round. You can make it whenever you want, too—if you're in a pinch, we give you permission to use frozen mango chunks. The recipe was inspired by Francesco, who used to make it for himself nearly every day for breakfast while living in Mexico City. When in season, we prefer using the golden, sun-kissed Ataulfo or champagne mango from Mexico, which has a sweet, almost buttery, juicy flesh that's less fibrous than other mango varieties. Freezing the mango cubes ahead of time ensures a cold smoothie and prevents the avocado from oxidizing.

SERVES 1

1 small mango, preferably Ataulfo, pitted, peeled, diced, and frozen

¼ avocado, pitted and peeled

1¼ cups unsweetened almond milk

1 teaspoon agave syrup

1 teaspoon fresh lime juice

1. In a blender, combine the frozen mango, avocado, almond milk, agave, and lime juice and blend on high speed until smooth, about 25 seconds.

vanilla-almond smoothie

Working long hours at the shop always has us reaching for something sweet, but we try to be careful of what we eat so that we maintain our energy levels and don't experience sugar spikes. Medjool dates add a rich, mellow sweetness to this smoothie while providing a natural energy boost—without the sugar crash—thanks to their high fiber content, while the salt from the almonds complements that sweetness. Want more creaminess? Add a dollop of plain Greek yogurt.

SERVES 1

1 tablespoon salted almonds

2 Medjool dates, pitted

1 teaspoon agave syrup

¼ teaspoon pure vanilla extract

1 cup unsweetened almond milk

½ avocado, pitted and peeled

½ cup ice cubes

1. In a blender, combine the almonds, dates, agave, vanilla, and almond milk and blend on high speed until smooth, about 25 seconds. Add the avocado and ice; blend again on high speed until smooth, about 25 seconds.

matcha-kale green smoothie

Avocado. Kale. Matcha. The nutty sweetness of the kale balances the full-bodied, umami-rich taste of matcha, and avocado brings it all together in this lusciously creamy superfood smoothie.

SERVES 1

2 cups loosely packed curly kale leaves

⅓ banana, peeled, diced, and frozen

¼ avocado, pitted and peeled

1½ cups unsweetened coconut milk (in a carton, not canned)

1 teaspoon agave syrup

¼ teaspoon matcha green tea powder

1. In a blender, combine the kale, frozen banana, avocado, coconut milk, agave, and matcha and blend on high speed until smooth, about 25 seconds.

raspberry, dragon fruit & lychee smoothie

This recipe is almost mythical not because of dragons (sorry, they're not real!), but because of how many nutrients we managed to cram into one flavor-packed smoothie. Dragon fruit, also known as pitaya, are super-rich in antioxidants, vitamin C, and fatty acids, while raspberries contain even more vitamin C plus manganese, which supports bone health and speeds up metabolism.

SERVES 1

½ cup frozen raspberries

½ cup frozen cubed red dragon fruit

1¼ cups lychee juice

2 teaspoons fresh lime juice

1 teaspoon agave syrup

1 tablespoon grated fresh ginger

¼ avocado, pitted and peeled

1. In a blender, combine the raspberries, dragon fruit, lychee juice, lime juice, agave, ginger, and avocado and blend on high speed until smooth, about 25 seconds.

mexican hot chocolate

We drank a loooooot of Mexican hot chocolate during our first New York City winter, which was brutal, to say the least. We would blend avocado into the hot chocolate to make it extra thick and creamy to up the comfort factor, while the warm spices were bracing and had us ready (well . . . almost) to go outside and do battle with the city's icy sidewalks.

SERVES 2

2 cups unsweetened rice milk or any nondairy milk

6 thin slices fresh red chile, preferably medium spicy such as red Fresno

1 tablespoon dark brown sugar

½ teaspoon ground cinnamon

½ teaspoon ground ginger

¼ cup chocolate chips, preferably 60% cacao, chopped

2 tablespoons unsweetened cocoa powder

1 avocado, pitted, peeled, and chopped

1. In a small saucepan, combine the rice milk, chile, brown sugar, cinnamon, and ginger and heat over low heat until hot, but not boiling. Remove from the heat and discard the chile. Add the chopped chocolate and cacao powder. Using an immersion blender, blend until smooth. Add the avocado; blend until smooth and creamy. Serve immediately.

avo-colada smoothie

A twist on the tropical cocktail, our smoothie won't exactly get you drunk for lunch—most of the alcohol actually cooks off. Hosting an avo party? Stir in an extra splash of good-quality rum before serving. Oh, and our housemade rum syrup isn't just for smoothies—drizzle any leftover syrup over our avo pancakes (page 28) or your favorite ice cream.

SERVES 2

FOR THE RUM SYRUP

¼ cup aged rum

¼ cup packed dark brown sugar

¼ cup granulated sugar

¼ teaspoon ground allspice

FOR THE SMOOTHIE

2 cups fresh pineapple cubes, plus 2 pineapple wedges for serving

½ avocado, pitted and peeled

1½ cups unsweetened canned full-fat coconut milk

12 ice cubes, plus more for serving

2 tablespoons aged rum (optional)

1. **MAKE THE SYRUP:** In a medium saucepan, combine the rum, brown sugar, granulated sugar, allspice, and ¼ cup water and bring to a boil over medium heat. Reduce the heat and simmer, stirring occasionally, until the sugar has dissolved, about 3 minutes. Remove from the heat and let cool completely.

2. **MAKE THE SMOOTHIE:** In a blender, combine ¼ cup of the rum syrup, the pineapple, avocado, coconut milk, ice cubes, and rum (if using) and blend on high speed until smooth and creamy, about 30 seconds.

3. Serve in 2 glasses filled with ice cubes and garnish each with a pineapple wedge. Store any remaining rum syrup in an airtight container in the refrigerator for up to 1 month.

TIP:
This pineapple-packed smoothie is an immunity booster. Just a ½-cup serving of this tropical fruit has more than 130 percent of the daily requirement of vitamin C.

spreads +
toppings

pistachio dukkah

Dukkah is an Egyptian nut-and-spice blend that we sprinkle over toasts, salads, and grain bowls. Hazelnuts are classically the preferred nut, but we like to add pistachios for more crunch and depth of flavor.

MAKES 2 CUPS

1½ cups shelled salted roasted pistachios
½ cup dukkah spice blend

1. In a food processor, pulse the pistachios until coarsely chopped. Transfer to a medium bowl and stir in the dukkah. Store in a resealable container at room temperature for up to 2 weeks.

spiced seeds

We like to sprinkle these on our toasts and salads for flavor and an unexpected crunch. To make this recipe, we toast a mix of seeds with the North African spice blend ras el hanout, which imparts a warm, aromatic taste and deepens the flavor. After a few minutes over the heat, you'll know the seeds are ready when you hear them start to pop.

MAKES 2 CUPS

1½ teaspoons olive oil
1 cup flaxseeds, preferably a mix of brown and golden
½ cup hulled pumpkin seeds
½ cup hulled sunflower seeds
1½ teaspoons ras el hanout spice blend
Salt

1. Set a rimmed baking sheet on a wire rack and line the baking sheet with paper towels. In a large nonstick skillet, heat the olive oil over medium heat until hot but not smoking. Stir in the flaxseeds, pumpkin seeds, sunflower seeds, and ras el hanout; cook, stirring continuously, until the seeds are toasted and golden, 4 to 5 minutes. Remove from the heat and sprinkle with salt; transfer to the prepared baking sheet and let cool. Store in a resealable container at room temperature for up to 1 week.

croutons

At our shop, we make hundreds of toasts daily. With any leftover bread—which often means lots of loaf ends—we make our extra-crispy croutons. You can also grind the croutons in a food processor to make toasted bread crumbs, which are versatile and can be sprinkled over just about everything for added texture (think roasted veggies, gratins, casseroles, etc.).

MAKES ABOUT 2 CUPS

3 thick-cut bread slices, cut into 1-inch cubes (about 2 cups)
1 tablespoon olive oil
¼ teaspoon salt

1. Preheat the oven to 375°F.

2. In a large bowl, toss together the bread cubes, olive oil, and salt. Transfer to a rimmed baking sheet and bake until golden brown, about 8 minutes. Place on a wire rack and let cool.

3. Store the croutons in a resealable container at room temperature for up to 1 week.

cashew parmesan

Sure, someone in Italy is crying at the scandal of a nut-based parmesan, but we love our umami-packed alternative to the classic aged Italian cheese. We use this vegan parm to top our Avo Caesar (page 76). The key to the recipe is the nutritional yeast, a deactivated yeast made from sugarcane and beet molasses that has a nutty, cheesy flavor and is packed with B vitamins.

MAKES 2 CUPS

1⅓ cups unsalted roasted cashews
⅔ cup nutritional yeast
1 tablespoon salt

1. In a food processor, combine the cashews, yeast, and salt and pulse until the cashews are coarsely chopped and the mixture resembles finely grated Parmesan cheese. Store the cashew parm in a resealable container at room temperature for up to 2 months.

avo-coconut granola

We often top our chocolate mousse (page 146) with this granola, which lends it a nice crunch. You could also eat this as a healthy snack all by itself.

MAKES 6 CUPS

2 cups oat flakes or rolled oats

2 cups puffed quinoa

1 cup unsweetened coconut flakes

½ cup puffed spelt or Kamut

½ cup mixed seeds, such as hulled pumpkin seeds, hulled sunflower seeds, flaxseeds, chia seeds, and/or hemp seeds

2 tablespoons granulated coconut sugar

2 tablespoons avocado oil

2 tablespoons coconut oil

3 tablespoons molasses

1. Preheat the oven to 350°F.

2. In a large bowl, mix together the oat flakes, quinoa, coconut flakes, spelt, seeds, coconut sugar, and avocado oil. Spread evenly on a rimmed baking sheet and bake until golden, about 15 minutes; let cool to room temperature. Reduce the oven temperature to 300°F.

3. Meanwhile, in a small saucepan, melt the coconut oil over low heat. Remove from the heat and stir in the molasses until combined. Drizzle the mixture over the baked granola and toss to evenly coat; return the granola to the oven and bake until crunchy, about 15 minutes. Let cool to room temperature.

4. Store the granola in resealable containers at room temperature for up to 2 weeks.

vegan chicharrónes

One day after eating avocados and vegetables nonstop, Alberto wanted something meaty-tasting and picked up two bags of pork chicharrónes from one of the Mexican bodegas in Sunset Park. It was the first time he had ever tasted pork rinds, and he was hooked—he ate them all in about, oh, three minutes flat. That experience inspired him to develop this healthier, plant-based version. Liquid smoke gives these guys their "meaty" flavor. To get the traditional texture, he dehydrates sheets of tapioca-based batter, breaks them into pieces, and flash-fries them until golden. We like to use these chicharrónes to scoop up guacamole (pages 122 and 125).

MAKES 10

1 cup small tapioca pearls
2 teaspoons liquid smoke
1 teaspoon salt
1 teaspoon garam masala
1 teaspoon tandoori spice blend
Vegetable oil, for frying

1. Preheat the oven to 175°F. Line two baking sheets with parchment paper.

2. Place the tapioca pearls, liquid smoke, salt, garam masala, tandoori spice blend, and 3 cups water in a medium saucepan; cook over medium heat, whisking, until the tapioca pearls have dissolved, about 25 minutes.

3. Evenly spread a thin layer of the tapioca mixture over each prepared baking sheet. Bake until dry, about 6 hours. Break into 5 x 2-inch pieces and store in resealable containers for up to 3 days.

4. When ready to use, fill a large pot with vegetable oil to a depth of about 3 inches. Heat the oil to 350°F. Line a couple of baking sheets with paper towels and have them nearby. Working in batches, fry the tapioca pieces until golden, about 3 seconds. Use a slotted spoon to transfer the chicharrónes to the paper towels to drain and let cool to room temperature. Store at room temperature in an airtight container for up to 3 days.

beet hummus

For our first menu, we tested out hummus and arugula as toppings for a vegan toast, but something was missing. Then we added some pureed beets to the hummus and were instantly amazed at not only the beautiful pink color, but at how the sweetness from the beets brightened up the earthy hummus. To make the smoothest, creamiest hummus, we always skin the chickpeas, which is easier than you'd think. Just rinse the chickpeas under cold water, then shell them using your hands—the skins will slide right off.

MAKES 2 CUPS

FOR THE BEET PUREE

1 medium beet, cooked, peeled, and diced (see page 74), 1 cup cooking water reserved

FOR THE CHICKPEA HUMMUS

1 (15.5-ounce) can chickpeas, drained, rinsed, and preferably skinned (see note above)

2 tablespoons olive oil

2 tablespoons fresh lemon juice

1 tablespoon tahini

2 tablespoons salt

¼ teaspoon ras el hanout spice blend

1. **MAKE THE BEET PUREE:** Combine the beet and the reserved cooking water in a blender and puree on high speed until smooth. You should have about ¾ cup beet puree.

2. **MAKE THE HUMMUS:** In a blender, combine the chickpeas, olive oil, lemon juice, tahini, salt, and ras el hanout and blend on high speed until smooth. You should have about 1¼ cups hummus.

3. Add the beet puree and blend on high speed until combined.

4. Store the beet hummus in a resealable container and keep refrigerated for up to 5 days.

yogurt & fresh herbs

We use this simple, rich yogurt mixture as a spread or dressing on our salads and in soups and main dishes. If you want a more salad dressing–like consistency, just add water, 1 tablespoon at a time. For a tzatziki-style flavor, stir in some grated cucumbers and garlic.

MAKES ABOUT 1½ CUPS

1 cup plus 2 tablespoons
   plain Greek yogurt
2½ tablespoons infused
   olive oil from Olive Oil &
   Herb dressing (page 190)
2 teaspoons salt

1. In a bowl, combine the yogurt, dressing, salt, and ¼ cup water and whisk until combined. Store in a resealable container in the refrigerator for up to 5 days.

olive tapenade

We spread this incredibly versatile French condiment on our Mediterranean toast (page 49), but you can also stir it into hummus, spread it over pizza crust, or toss it with roasted vegetables.

MAKES 2 CUPS

1 heaping cup pitted
   Kalamata olives in brine,
   drained, 1 cup brine
   reserved
¼ cup capers, drained
2½ tablespoons olive oil

1. In a blender, combine the olives, olive brine, capers, and olive oil and blend on high speed until combined. Store the tapenade in a resealable container in the refrigerator for up to 1 week.

TIP:
You'll notice that we use capers in many of our recipes, but do you actually know what capers are? Although you might think capers are weird-looking peas, they're actually the flower buds of the caper bush, otherwise known as the Flinders rose. Capers are dried in the sun and later brined or pickled. They add a delicious, salty tang to some of our favorite recipes and we throw these guys on all kinds of savory stuff to further enhance flavor.

green pico

This isn't your traditional pico de gallo, but we promise it delivers on flavor. We swapped in subtle-flavored ingredients—cucumber, celery, and jicama—for the usual tomato, onion, and chile, making it more versatile for use in other recipes.

MAKES 2 CUPS

⅔ cup ¼-inch cubes cucumber
⅔ cup ¼-inch cubes celery
⅔ cup ¼-inch cubes jicama

1. In a medium bowl, toss together the cucumber, celery, and jicama. Store the pico in a resealable container in the refrigerator for up to 5 days.

mango-corn salsa

Sometimes simple is all you need, especially when you're working with fresh produce in the summertime. Find the best corn, tomato, and mango you can and let the ingredients do the talking. We pair this with our chia-crusted tuna (page 118) but it would go with just about anything—we challenge you to find something this doesn't taste good with!

MAKES 2 CUPS

⅓ cup pico de gallo (see page 130), with some juices
½ fresh mango, cut into ¼-inch cubes (⅓ cup)
⅓ cup cooked fresh corn kernels

1. In a small bowl, stir together the pico de gallo, mango, and corn. Store in an airtight container in the refrigerator for up to 3 days.

pecan chermoula

Our version of this traditional garlicky North African sauce, packed with fresh herbs and spices, swaps in lemon juice for preserved lemon. We also add a little sweetness and crunch with pecans. We use chermoula to top toasts like Za'atar & Lemon (page 56) and soups like Cauliflower Velouté (page 88).

MAKES 1 CUP

⅓ cup olive oil

1 clove garlic, crushed

¼ teaspoon ground cumin

¼ teaspoon ground coriander

1 cup fresh parsley leaves with tender stems

½ cup fresh cilantro leaves with tender stems

¼ cup pecans

1 teaspoon finely grated lemon zest

2 tablespoons fresh lemon juice

¼ teaspoon salt

1. In a small saucepan, heat the olive oil until hot but not smoking. Remove from the heat and add the garlic, cumin, and coriander; let cool to room temperature. Transfer to a food processor and add the parsley, cilantro, pecans, lemon zest, lemon juice, and salt; process until coarsely chopped, about 25 seconds. Store in an airtight container in the refrigerator for up to 3 days.

**VARIATION
AVO-CHERMOULA DIP**

Place 1 cup chermoula in a food processor with 1 small pitted and peeled avocado. Pulse until the dip reaches a chunky consistency. Serve immediately.

dressings + sauces

olive oil & herb

Infusing warm olive oil with herbs is easy and is a great flavor booster. We use it in our Yogurt & Fresh Herbs dressing (page 185), and it's perfect as a replacement for plain olive oil in most recipes, like roasted vegetables and meats.

MAKES 1 ⅓ CUPS

2 cups olive oil
2 tablespoons fresh mint leaves
2 tablespoons fresh thyme leaves
2 tablespoons fresh rosemary

1. In a large pot, heat the olive oil over medium heat until hot but not smoking. Remove from the heat and submerge the mint, thyme, and rosemary in the oil; let cool to room temperature. Using an immersion blender, blend the oil and herbs for 15 to 20 seconds, then strain out the herbs and store the infused oil in a resealable container in the refrigerator for up to 1 week.

lime citronette

It's true that the ratio for salad dressing is typically 3 parts oil to 1 part acid, but we tweak ours closer to 4 parts oil to 1 part acid for a less acidic, more balanced flavor. Adding xanthan gum—a natural food additive that can be found in the baking section of most grocery stores or online—helps stabilize the emulsion of olive oil and lime juice, giving the dressing its light, velvety texture (but it's optional if you don't have it on hand).

MAKES ABOUT 1 ½ CUPS

¼ cup fresh lime juice (from about 10 limes)
1 tablespoon salt
⅛ teaspoon xanthan gum (optional)
1 cup olive oil

1. In a blender, combine the lime juice, salt, xanthan gum (if using), and ¼ cup water and blend on high speed until combined, about 20 seconds. With the motor running, stream in the olive oil until combined, about 20 seconds. Store the dressing in resealable containers in the refrigerator for up to 1 week.

agave mustard dressing

When we first opened the shop, we made a traditional honey mustard dressing, but because we have so many vegan customers, we decided to swap in agave syrup for the honey. And guess what? It's just as good, if not better. Try dunking baked avo (page 31) in this mustard for happy results.

¼ cup agave syrup

2 tablespoons apple cider vinegar

1 tablespoon Dijon mustard

1 tablespoon salt

½ teaspoon black pepper

⅛ teaspoon xanthan gum (optional)

1 cup olive oil

1. In a blender, combine the agave, vinegar, mustard, salt, pepper, xanthan gum (if using), and 2 tablespoons water and blend on high speed until combined, about 20 seconds. With the motor running, stream in the olive oil until combined, about 20 seconds. Store the dressing in resealable containers in the refrigerator for up to 1 week.

raspberry balsamic

In an attempt to capture the sweet-and-sour fruitiness of traditional balsamic vinegar from Alessandro's native city of Modena, Italy, Alberto combined the unusual flavors of raspberries, beets, and hibiscus water with some apple cider vinegar.

MAKES 1¼ CUPS

¼ cup frozen raspberries

2 tablespoons chopped cooked beets (see page 74)

1½ tablespoons apple cider vinegar

¼ cup hibiscus water (see page 53)

1 tablespoon agave syrup

1 tablespoon molasses

1 tablespoon salt

¼ teaspoon xanthan gum (optional)

½ cup olive oil

¼ cup canola oil

1. In a blender, combine the raspberries, beets, vinegar, hibiscus water, agave, molasses, salt, xanthan gum (if using), and 2 tablespoons water and blend on high speed until smooth, about 30 seconds. With the motor running on low speed, slowly stream in the olive oil and canola oil until combined, about 30 seconds. Store the dressing in a resealable container in the refrigerator for up to 1 week.

vegan avo caesar dressing

Alberto replaced the typical anchovies and Parmesan cheese with capers and green peppercorns, which are lacto-fermented—one of the oldest methods of pickling foods using beneficial bacteria. Translation? You get plenty of salty, briny flavor up in here, with countless benefits to boot, like warding off inflammation.

MAKES ABOUT 1 ¼ CUPS

1 tablespoon drained green peppercorns in brine
1 tablespoon Dijon mustard
1½ teaspoons drained capers
2 small cloves roasted garlic (see below)
1 cup Vegan Soy Mayo (page 196)

1. Place the peppercorns, mustard, capers, garlic, 2½ teaspoons water, and the mayo in a medium bowl. Using an immersion blender, blend until combined, about 10 seconds. Store the dressing in a resealable container in the refrigerator for up to 1 week.

HOW TO: Roast Garlic

1. Preheat the oven to 400°F.

2. Place whole cloves of garlic on a sheet of aluminum foil and add fresh herbs, a generous drizzle of olive oil, and a pinch of salt. Wrap in the foil and set on a small baking sheet.

3. Roast until the garlic cloves are golden and softened, about 12 minutes.

tomato-herb dressing

Charred tomatoes are the base for this dressing, which we use in our Avo Tabbouleh Bowl (page 84). Alberto developed the recipe with the earthy flavors of Middle Eastern foods in mind—especially the tomatoes, inspired by the char-grilled meat-and-vegetable kebabs he ate in Istanbul.

MAKES ABOUT 2 CUPS

2 cups fresh parsley leaves
¼ cup fresh mint leaves
¼ cup fresh basil leaves
4 medium tomatoes
3 tablespoons chopped scallions
2 tablespoons plus 2 teaspoons fresh lemon juice
1 tablespoon salt

1. Fill a large bowl with ice and water. Bring a saucepan of salted water to a boil. Add the parsley, mint, and basil and blanch for 1 minute. Using a slotted spoon, immediately transfer the herbs to the ice bath.

2. Meanwhile, preheat the broiler and line a baking sheet with foil. Set the tomatoes on the baking sheet and broil until charred, about 15 minutes. (Alternatively, if you have one, you can use a blowtorch to char the tomatoes.) Let cool, then coarsely chop the tomatoes and transfer to a blender.

3. Place the scallions in a separate ice bath for 10 minutes; drain and transfer to the blender with the chopped tomatoes. Add the parsley, mint, basil, lemon juice and salt. Blend until smooth.

guaca mayo

Why have regular mayo when you can have avocado mayo? Who's with us, right?! And before you ask, the answer is yes, we have used this on top of avocado, and it's delicious. We have no regrets. The lime juice stops the avocado from browning, but we still recommend enjoying this mayo within a day.

MAKES 1 CUP

1 avocado, pitted and peeled
2 tablespoons olive oil
2 tablespoons canola oil
2 teaspoons fresh lime juice
½ teaspoon salt

1. Place the avocado, olive oil, canola oil, lime juice, and salt in a medium bowl. Using an immersion blender, process until creamy, about 10 seconds. Store the mayo in a resealable container in the refrigerator for up to 1 week.

vegan chipotle & turmeric mayo

We call this our yin-and-yang dressing: Turmeric is cooling and anti-inflammatory, while chipotle peppers deliver their signature smoky, sweet heat. That said, we prefer to use canned chipotles in adobo sauce because they're milder and softer than fresh chiles. Want to turn up the heat? Use dried whole chiles (see note below). If you want a thinner mayo to use as a dressing, just whisk in water, 1 tablespoon at a time, until it reaches your desired consistency.

MAKES ABOUT 1 CUP

1 cup Vegan Soy Mayo (page 196)

1¾ teaspoons ground turmeric, or 1½ tablespoons finely grated peeled fresh turmeric

1½ tablespoons chopped chipotle peppers in adobo sauce

1. Place ½ cup of the mayo, the turmeric, and the chipotle peppers in a small bowl. Using an immersion blender (or use a mini food processor), blend until combined, about 10 seconds; fold in the remaining ½ cup mayo. Transfer to a squeeze bottle or resealable plastic bag with a tiny corner off before using. Store the mayo in the refrigerator for up to 1 week.

HOW TO: Cook with Dried Whole Chipotle Chiles

1. Toast the chiles in a dry skillet for 3 minutes.

2. Soak the toasted chiles in warm water for about 25 minutes.

3. Drain the chiles, then blend (in a blender, mini food processor, or using an immersion blender) with canola oil, 1 teaspoon at a time, until the mixture reaches a paste-like consistency.

vegan soy mayo

This mayo, which is lighter in texture and flavor than classic mayonnaise, can be used as a base for many different dressings. Make it your own by stirring in your favorite spices or herbs.

MAKES 1 CUP

⅓ cup unsweetened soy milk

2 tablespoons fresh lemon juice

¾ teaspoon salt

⅓ cup plus 2 tablespoons canola oil

1. Place the soy milk, lemon juice, and salt in a medium bowl. Using an immersion blender, blend until combined, about 10 seconds. With the motor running on low speed, slowly stream in the canola oil until the mayo is creamy and emulsified, about 20 seconds. Store the mayo in a resealable container in the refrigerator for up to 1 week.

1 Agave Mustard Dressing (page 191)   **2** Guaca Mayo (page 194)   **3** Lime Citronette (page 190)   **4** Vegan Chipotle & Turmeric Mayo (page 195)
5 Vegan Soy Mayo (page 196)   **6** Olive Oil & Herb (page 190)

resources

———

Can't find something at your local retailer? Just get it delivered right to your doorstep. Ah, the wonders of technology.

FORMAGGIO KITCHEN
formaggiokitchen.com
A unique shop specializing in local and international artisan and handmade foods, including small-production cheeses, pantry staples, and hard-to-find salts.

KALUSTYAN'S
foodsofnations.com
Think beyond Indian foods—the shop's origins—and you'll find an international mix of not just spices, but nuts, seeds, legumes, oils, grains, and even dried flowers for tea.

LA BOÎTE
laboiteny.com
Lior Lev Sercarz, the spice master of New York City, has been blending spices for chefs for decades. Now you can shop his selection of the best aromatic spices from around the world.

LE SANCTUAIRE
le-sanctuaire.mybigcommerce.com
Consider this site your culinary muse. You'll find rare ingredients, including spices, flowers, and berries, as well as high-quality emulsifiers and kitchen tools.

PENZEYS

penzeys.com

You've reached the spice mecca. 'Nuff said.

WORLD SPICE MERCHANTS

worldspice.com

For the past twenty years, this shop has supplied high-quality regional and international herbs, spices, and teas to chefs.

AMAZON

amazon.com

You're familiar with this giant online retailer. If you can't find something, there's a good chance it'll be available here.

say it: 21 funky italian expressions

———

EXPRESSION: *Come il cavolo a merenda*
LITERAL TRANSLATION: Like a cabbage at teatime
WHAT IT REALLY MEANS: When things don't go well together
USAGE IN A SENTENCE: "That cowboy hat doesn't really fit with Avocaderia's uniform—*come il cavolo a merenda!*"

EXPRESSION: *Avere grilli per la testa*
LITERAL TRANSLATION: To have crickets in the head
WHAT IT REALLY MEANS: When you're lost in your thoughts
USAGE IN A SENTENCE: "Francesco, why did you forget to add avocado to the salad? What do you have, *grilli per la testa*?!"

EXPRESSION: *Paese che vai usanza che trovi*
LITERAL TRANSLATION: Whatever country, you find different habits
WHAT IT REALLY MEANS: Every place does things differently
USAGE IN A SENTENCE: "In Mexico, they eat avocado straight up, with just a bit of lemon and salt. *Paese che vai usanza che trovi.*"

EXPRESSION: *Nato con la camicia*
LITERAL TRANSLATION: Born with his shirt on
WHAT IT REALLY MEANS: Elegant in what he or she does
USAGE IN A SENTENCE: "Avocaderia's cashier is such a gentleman, *é nato con la camicia.*"

EXPRESSION: *Non é l'abito che fa il monaco*
LITERAL TRANSLATION: Clothes don't make the monk
WHAT IT REALLY MEANS: Appearances don't matter
USAGE IN A SENTENCE: "Everyone is welcome at Avocaderia—*non é l'abito che fa il monaco.*"

EXPRESSION: *Non dire gatto finché non ce l'hai nel sacco*
LITERAL TRANSLATION: Don't say cat until you have it in the bag
WHAT IT REALLY MEANS: Be conservative until you reach your goal
USAGE IN A SENTENCE: "Since this book is so amazing, will you get another book deal? Well . . . *non dire gatto finché non ce l'hai nel sacco.*"

EXPRESSION: *Il lupo perde il pelo ma non il vizio*
LITERAL TRANSLATION: The wolf may lose his fur, but not his vice
WHAT IT REALLY MEANS: Old habits die hard
USAGE IN A SENTENCE: "You said you wouldn't eat more avocado mousse unless you went running, but there you go again! *Il lupo perde il pelo ma non il vizio.*"

EXPRESSION: *Gallina vecchia fa buon brodo*
LITERAL TRANSLATION: An old hen makes good broth
WHAT IT REALLY MEANS: There's a lot to learn from older people with more experience
USAGE IN A SENTENCE: "Alessandro, Francesco is technically one day older than you, so you should really listen to him. *Gallina vecchia fa buon brodo!*"

EXPRESSION: *Sui gusti non si disputa*
LITERAL TRANSLATION: One doesn't argue about tastes
WHAT IT REALLY MEANS: Everyone has different tastes
USAGE IN A SENTENCE: "Do you really want to add avocado to your coffee?! Well, okay, *sui gusti non si disputa!*"

EXPRESSION: *Ogni lasciata è persa*
LITERAL TRANSLATION: Everything left is lost
WHAT IT REALLY MEANS: Take your chances or you'll lose an opportunity
USAGE IN A SENTENCE: "We found an amazing location for Avocaderia in Chelsea, but it's a little expensive. What should we do? Go for it—*ogni lasciata è persa!*"

EXPRESSION: *Avere un chiodo fisso*
LITERAL TRANSLATION: To have a fixed nail
WHAT IT REALLY MEANS: To be obsessed with something
USAGE IN A SENTENCE: "We've heard a lot of customers say Alessandro is a total babe; he's their *chiodo fisso!*"

EXPRESSION: *Tutti i nodi vengono al pettine*
LITERAL TRANSLATION: All the knots get caught in the comb
WHAT IT REALLY MEANS: Your sins will find you
USAGE IN A SENTENCE: "It looked too good to be true—and it was! Remember, *tutti i nodi vengono al pettine.*"

EXPRESSION: *Non è sempre Domenica*
LITERAL TRANSLATION: It's not always Sunday
WHAT IT REALLY MEANS: Life isn't always easy
USAGE IN A SENTENCE: "I spent all day pitting avocados! *Non è sempre Domenica . . .*"

EXPRESSION: *La notte porta consiglio*
LITERAL TRANSLATION: The night brings advice
WHAT IT REALLY MEANS: Sleep on it
USAGE IN A SENTENCE: "Should we add another toast to our summer menu? Let's decide tomorrow—*la notte porta consiglio.*"

EXPRESSION: *Andar via come il pane*
LITERAL TRANSLATION: Vanish like bread
WHAT IT REALLY MEANS: When something sells out quickly
USAGE IN A SENTENCE: "On Avocaderia's opening day, we ran out of avocados—*sono andati via come il pane!*"

EXPRESSION: *Dacci un taglio!*
LITERAL TRANSLATION: Cut it out
WHAT IT REALLY MEANS: Give us a break
USAGE IN A SENTENCE: "Oh no, you're playing that lousy music in the store again? Francesco, please *dacci un taglio!*"

EXPRESSION: *Stare con le mani in mano*
LITERAL TRANSLATION: Be with your hands in hand
WHAT IT REALLY MEANS: Sit on your hands and do nothing
USAGE IN A SENTENCE: "Come on, Francesco, we need to clean the floor and open the shop. *Non stare con le mani in mano!*"

EXPRESSION: *Piove sul bagnato*
LITERAL TRANSLATION: It rains on the wet
WHAT IT REALLY MEANS: Something bad just got worse
USAGE IN A SENTENCE: "Oops, I forgot the keys to the restaurant and there's already a line of people waiting outside. *Piove sul bagnato!*"

EXPRESSION: *Non avere peli sulla lingua*
LITERAL TRANSLATION: Not having hair on the tongue
WHAT IT REALLY MEANS: Tell the truth
USAGE IN A SENTENCE: "Please share your honest feedback about this cookbook; *senza peli sulla lingua!*"

EXPRESSION: *Perdersi in un bicchiere d'acqua*
LITERAL TRANSLATION: To lose oneself in a glass of water
WHAT IT REALLY MEANS: To be confused
USAGE IN A SENTENCE: "I don't understand why this new oven doesn't turn on." "Did you plug it in first?" "Um, *mi sono perso in un bicchiere d'acqua!*"

EXPRESSION: *Meglio un uovo oggi che una gallina domani*
LITERAL TRANSLATION: Better an egg today than a hen tomorrow
WHAT IT REALLY MEANS: Choose what you know to be true today over tomorrow's unknown
USAGE IN A SENTENCE: "Should we take the investment proposal from the Sharks or wait for a better one? Take it: *Meglio un uovo oggi che una gallina domani.*"

avocaderia playlist

---

1. "Let's Dance" – David Bowie

2. "A Change Is Gonna Come" – Sam Cooke

3. "Wouldn't It Be Nice"– Beach Boys

4. "This Must Be the Place" – Talking Heads

5. "Stay with Me Baby" – Duffy

6. "Father and Son" – Cat Stevens

7. "Dancing in the Street" – Martha & The Vandellas

8. "My Generation" – The Who

9. "You Can't Always Get What You Want" – The Rolling Stones

10. "Friday on My Mind" – The Easybeats

11. "I'm Alive" – The Hollies

12. "Baby Love" – The Supremes

13. "The Wind Cries Mary" – Jimi Hendrix

14. "For Your Love" – The Yardbirds

15. "Land of 1000 Dances" – Wilson Pickett

16. "Lazy Sunday" – Small Faces

17. "Rock Steady" – Aretha Franklin

18. "This Old Heart of Mine" – The Isley Brothers

19. "(Sittin' On) The Dock of the Bay" – Otis Redding

20. "Try a Little Tenderness" – Otis Redding

21. "Victoria" – The Kinks

22. "Ain't No Mountain High Enough" – Marvin Gaye and Tammi Terrell

23. "Feeling Good" – Nina Simone

24. "At Last" – Etta James

25. "Like a Rolling Stone" – Bob Dylan

26. "A Day in the Life" – The Beatles

27. "Be My Baby" – The Ronettes

28. "God Only Knows" – The Beach Boys

29. "Walk on the Wild Side" – Lou Reed

30. "Gimme Shelter" – The Rolling Stones

31. "Sunday Morning" – The Velvet Underground

32. "These Boots Are Made for Walkin'" – Nancy Sinatra

33. "See Emily Play" – Pink Floyd

34. "What a Wonderful World" – Louis Armstrong

35. "Whiter Shade of Pale" – Procol Harum

36. "Space Oddity" – David Bowie

Bonus Tracks

"Mis Sentimientos" - Los Ángeles Azules ft. Ximena Sariñana

"Amore Disperato" - Nada

"

We change our playlist—just like our menu—with the seasons.

"

menu ideas

New Year's Eve
- Avo Burger (page 96)
- Avo-Chocolate Mousse (page 146)
- Let It Beet toasts (page 50; make them mini)

Summer Picnic
- Greek Island Salad (page 68)
- Ginger-Mint Lemonade (page 168)
- Avo-Lime Cheesecake (page 153)
- Avo Tuna Tostada bar (page 53)

Super Bowl
- Traditional Guac (page 122)
- Guac Tots with Pico de Gallo (page 130)
- Baja Fish Tacos (page 119)

Brunch
- Chill Out Toast with Egg (page 40)
- El Salmon (page 46)
- Matcha-Kale Green Smoothie (page 173)
- Upside-Down Avo-Banana Cake with Coconut Caramel (page 36)

Birthday

- Avo Burger (page 96)
- Signature Guac with pita chips (page 125)
- Avo-Chocolate Mousse (page 146)

Avocaderia's Birthday (April 10)

- Tons of guac (page 122 or 125)
- Champagne

Cocktail Party

- Avo Deviled Eggs (page 141)
- Avo "Seed" Chocolate Truffles (page 148)
- Pinzimonio with Blue Cheese–Avo Dip (page 133)

Italian Holiday

- Mediterranean Toast (page 49)
- Zucchini Spaghetti with Avo Pesto (page 104)
- Avo Paletas (page 157)

vegan recipes

vegetarian (ovo-lacto) recipes

All vegan recipes at left plus:

Avo Pancakes with Blueberries & Ginger Syrup (page 28)

Chill Out Toast with Egg (page 40)

Avo Yogurt Mousse (page 43)

Upside-Down Avo-Banana Cake with Coconut Caramel (page 36)

Mediterranean Toast (page 49)

Green Peas, Mint & Burrata Toast (page 58)

Mozzarella & Avo Pesto Melt (page 62)

Greek Island Salad (page 68)

Beets & Blue (page 74)

Watermelon Salad (page 79)

Cauliflower Velouté (page 88)

Chilled Cucumber Soup (page 91)

Avo-Falafel Burger (page 99)

Stuffed Avo with Puffed Quinoa and Spiced Crust (page 129)

Avo Deviled Eggs (page 141)

Grilled Corn with Avocado, Smoked Chipotle & Lemon Butter (page 143)

Avo-Lime Cheesecake (page 153)

Spread the Love Shortbread Cookie Thins (page 154)

No-Churn Avo Ice Cream (page 158)

Avo-Chocolate Sponge Cake with Mint-Avo Whipped Cream (page 160)

Caramelized Avocado Wedges with Spiced Seeds & Dulce de Leche (page 163)

Yogurt & Fresh Herbs (page 185)

gluten-free recipes

lists of vegan, vegetarian + gluten-free recipes

acknowledgments

WE WOULD LIKE to thank our mamme, papa, and our siblings (especially Bonza), who believed in Avocaderia since the first day we told them about the idea.

Thanks to our agent, Katherine Latshaw, who encouraged us to write the book and followed us along for the journey. We are deeply grateful to our publisher, Houghton Mifflin Harcourt, and editor, Stephanie Fletcher, for this opportunity and for being very supportive.

A special mention goes to Liza Zusman, who was able to keep everyone focused on the common goal of creating something beautiful.

To photographer Henry Hargreaves, food stylist Caitlin Levin, book designer Allison Chi, and cover designer Anna Resmini, who translated our ideas into art.

To writer Silvana Nardone, who did a precious job of infusing our Italian identity into the book.

To the Avocaderia crew, who prepares delicious food every day and serves it with a smile.

To avocados—the delicious fruit with countless health benefits that allowed us to create a global movement to inspire a happier, healthier lifestyle.

Lastly, and probably most importantly, we are forever beholden to all Avo Lovers!

We are Avo Lovers.
Avo Lovers don't belong to any gender, religion, race, or social group.

Avo Lovers are passionate about real food, live a sustainable life, and inspire others to improve their lifestyle.

Avo Lovers are enthusiasts, full of life, and ready to go the extra mile.

Avo Lovers believe in a healthy and happy lifestyle, and are aware of sacrifice without saying no to the pleasures of life.

Avo Lovers are a community of smilers, who see the beauty in the world and help others see that same beauty.

Avo Lovers are driven by curiosity, are eager to try new things, but are respectful of tradition.

This book is for you and we hope you enjoy it as much as we did bringing it to life.